WITH THE AFGHANS

WITH THE AFGHANS

CLAUD FIELD

GYAN

Published by

Gyan Publishing House
5, Ansari Road
Daryaganj, New Delhi-110002
Phone: 011-47034999, 9811692060
E-mail: books@gyanbooks.com

Distribution Network
gyanbooks.com
India, USA, Canada, UK, Australia

ISBN: 978-93-7447-616-1 (PB)

First Published, 1908

2nd Impression 2026

Printed at: Gyan Press, Delhi.

WITH THE AFGHANS
Author: CLAUD FIELD

WITH THE AFGHANS

A Street in a Native City.

WITH THE AFGHANS

BY

CLAUD FIELD, M A

Author of "Heroes of Missionary Enterprise" (Late C.M.S. Missionary at Peshawar)

WITH ILLUSTRATIONS AND MAP

PREFACE

AS the train toils slowly along the thousand miles from Bombay to the North-West Frontier at Peshawar and approaches the terminus, one becomes aware of a different type of native entering the carriages to the mild Hindoo. Stalwart bearded men over six feet high and clad, if it be winter, in "posteens," *i.e.*, rough sheep skins worn with the hair inwards, stalk up and down the platforms as if they and not the English were the lords of the country. These are the Pathans or Afghans, an attempt to describe mission work among whom is made in the following pages.

This mission work has been slow in commencing, and has proceeded amidst great difficulties. It is nearly a hundred years since William Carey, at Calcutta, employed a Pathan Munshi to translate the New Testament into Pushtu (1818). As one looks at the coarse paper and bad print, one is astonished at the far-seeing faith of the great Baptist missionary, for at that time the English Frontier had not touched the Panjab, and it was not till 1849 that that vast territory was annexed, nor till 1853 that the Peshawar mission was founded. In the latter year the Rev. Robert Clark, of the Church Missionary Society, arrived in Peshawar. He at once realised the immense strategic importance of the place in the missionary campaign, and that it was principally from

Preface

Peshawar that the Gospel was destined to penetrate into Afghanistan and Central Asia. His anticipations are now, more than half a century afterwards, being fulfilled, chiefly by the agency of the medical missions at Peshawar and Bannu, to which numerous tribesmen resort from trans-frontier districts, and from which they are known, in more than one instance, to have carried the Gospel message back to their fellow-countrymen.

Politically Afghanistan is still a closed country, and no missionary is allowed to cross the frontier, but as Abdur-rahman, the Afghan poet, says:—

"Na ba shi tarali pa *zanzir* sara hawā,"

"No chain can bind the wind,"

and the Gospel goes where the missionary cannot. The writer well remembers a young Afghan from Ningrahar, beyond the frontier, telling him that the first time he had come in contact with the Gospel was by someone having brought a torn copy of St. Matthew from Peshawar to his remote village.

As regards the type of convert made from among the Pathans, unsatisfactory as some doubtless are, the writer can only say that having worked nine years among the lower classes in London and nine in Peshawar, he has never among the former seen converts of such "grit" and character as he saw in what has been perhaps not unjustly termed "the vilest city in Asia."* The very darkness of the background throws such characters into strong and bright relief. C. F.

* "Blackwood's Magazine," 1879.

CONTENTS

LIST OF ILLUSTRATIONS

PREFATORY NOTE

MY best thanks are due to the Editor of the "Church Missionary Review" for permission to use material from the Church Missionary publications, and for the loan of photographs. Other photographs have been lent by private friends. Dr. Hastings has kindly allowed the inclusion of a paper which appeared in the "Expository Times."

C. F.

The Afghans: Their Origin and History The Ameer Abdurrahman

CHAPTER I

A WRITER on the Afghans is at once confronted with the question of their origin. According to their own tradition they are "Bani Israel," children of Israel, and trace their descent back to Afghana, said to be the commander-in-chief of King Solomon. Wild as this assertion may appear at first sight, Dr. Bellew, who resided for years in Afghanistan, and made a careful study of the people, is inclined to credit it. He adduces in support of his position the striking fact that many of their customs are not enjoined by their religion, Islam, and have a striking resemblance to Jewish ones. Thus at a time of pestilence it is a common thing to slaughter a sheep and sprinkle the blood on the door-posts, or to lead a heifer round the village, and then dismiss it into the wilderness. Their lands are periodically distributed by lot, and a widow becomes the wife of her deceased husband's brother. The striking Jewish cast of countenance which they nearly all possess lends considerable countenance to this theory.

On the other hand, linguistic experts like Dr. Trumpp have pronounced their language Pukhtu or Pushtu to be unmistakably Aryan, not semitic. The term Pukhtun (or Pathan, as the natives of India pronounce it) is probably derived from "Pukhta," a mountain ridge, and therefore properly applies to these hill-dwellers. Dr. Bellew identifies it with the Pactiyes mentioned by Herodotus. It is a term of wider range than Afghan. Every Afghan is a Pathan, but not every Pathan is an Afghan, just as every Scotchman or Welshman ranks as an Englishman, but every Englishman is not a Scotchman or Welshman. Thus the Hazara tribe, though of Mongol descent, count as Afghans, since they reside in the same country. Besides the explanation of the name Afghan given above, another is that this word, which in Persian means "lamentation," was applied to this people by reason of their constantly lamenting their deportation from their ancient home in Syria.

The name "Pathan" is said to have been given by Mohammed to Kais, the ancestor of the Afghans, when he went with some of the Afghan elders to Arabia to enquire into the truth of Islam. The term "Pathan" means in the Syrian language the rudder of a ship, Mohammed implying by it that Kais would guide his people in the right way. At any rate, the Afghans seem from an early date to have become zealous supporters of Islam, as they are to this date. Their earliest appearance in history is in the Suleiman mountains, in the district of Ghor, on the west of Afghanistan. In the eleventh century Mahmud of Ghazni enlisted Afghan auxiliaries in his repeated descents upon the rich plains of Hindustan. When he took Lahore and Delhi he is said to have left some Afghans settled there to spread Islam. After the death of Mahmoud, Bahram, one of his successors, put to death with great cruelty an Afghan prince of Ghor, Kutb-ud-din Sur. His death was avenged by Ala-ud-din, his brother, who utterly destroyed Ghazni, at that time one of the most magnificent cities in Asia. Ala-ud-din became the founder of the Afghan dynasty of the House of Ghor. His son, Shahab-ud-din, founded the Mahommedan empire in India after crushing the Rajputs (A.D. 1193). During the continual political upheavals which subsequently took place, several Afghan chiefs carved out kingdoms for themselves in Bengal and Orissa. In the fifteenth century the Afghan dynasty of Lodi obtained possession of the throne of Delhi itself. This dynasty was in its turn overthrown by the Emperor Baber (A.D. 1526), founder of the Moghul empire.

While Afghan adventurers were seeking their fortunes in India, the bulk of the nation remained in the mountains. Properly speaking, it was not a nation but a congeries of peoples, the Ghilzais being of Turkish, the Hazaras of Mongol origin, the Abdalis being genuine Afghans. The basis of the Afghan character is personal independence, and the fact of the various tribes possessing common customs as Muhammadans, instead of leading to the establishment of an ordered form of government, has only resulted for the most part in internecine warfare. Each tribe lives apart, its chief contact with neighbouring tribes being for purposes of cattle-lifting, and being itself torn by intestine quarrels.

At the commencement of the eighteenth century Herat and Candahar were under Persian influence; Cabul and Ghazni under Moghal. The two most important tribes were the Abdalis and the Ghilzais; the former in the region of Herat, the latter in that of Candahar. From this period onward the history of the Afghans is the history of the successive dominations of Ghilzais and Abdalis. Both had thrown off the Persian yoke till it was reimposed on them by Nadir Shah, the conqueror of Delhi. The army with which he invaded India included 16,000 Afghans, 4,000 of whom were Ghilzais, and 12,000 Abdalis.

After the assassination of Nadir Shah by a Persian soldier, a young Abdali, named Ahmed Khan, the hereditary chief of the clan of the Sadouzais, called on the

Afghans to avenge Nadir against the Persian troops who were all concerned in the plot for his assassination. Finding his forces outnumbered, he retired in good order upon Candahar, carrying with him the Koh-i-noor and pillaging on the way a caravan which was conveying to Nadir Shah the tribute of India, amounting to several lacs of rupees. Ahmed Khan was acclaimed king by his followers, and took the title of Ahmed Shah "*Durrani*," or "Pearl of the Age," a name by which his descendants have been known ever since. Ahmed Shah was the ideal of an Afghan king. He respected the independence of the tribes and led them four times to pillage India. He took Delhi, and annexed the Panjab, Scinde, and Kashmir. At his death the Durrani empire extended from Herat to the Sutlej, and from Bactria to the Indian Ocean.

In 1761 the Moghal Empire began to go to pieces. The Mahrattas, the warlike Hindus from the south, rose in rebellion and made the Great Mogol prisoner at Delhi. India was on the point of falling under Hindu domination when Ahmed Shah appeared on the scene with his Afghan forces reinforced by Moghal troops. The two armies met at Paniput, 250,000 Hindus and 200,000 Moslems. The Mahratta army was destroyed and the Mahratta Empire annihilated. India was at the feet of Ahmed Shah and the Mogol crown in his grasp. He ignored them both, feeling that the destiny of his race was to destroy not to organise. He had the courage to be moderate, and returned to Candahar laden with spoil, leaving behind him, as Darmesteter says, "the wrecks of two empires and India for the first comer to seize. The English merchants of Madras took forty years to guess this state secret."

The Durrani empire dissolved after the death of Ahmed Shah. The history of his three successors, Timour

(1773), Zeman Shah (1793), Mahmoud Shah (1800), is only that of continuous dismemberment. They renounced his policy and tried to curb the independence of the tribes, a step which gave rise to numerous conspiracies and civil wars. Mahmoud Shah passed his reign in defending himself against a pertinacious rival, his uncle Shah Shuja. He finally triumphed owing to the capability and resource of his minister Fateh Khan, chief of the Barukzai tribe, whom he rewarded by first blinding, and then having him cut in pieces. This was the signal for the fall of the Sadouzai dynasty.

The eleven brothers of Fateh Khan rose to avenge him, and put Mahmoud Shah to death. They then divided Afghanistan between themselves, taking the simple title of Sardars (chiefs). After thirty years of intestine wars, intrigues, and murders, during which the brothers allied themselves in turns with the Persians, the English, and the Sikhs, Dost Mohammed, the most energetic and able of the Barukzai Sardars, brought all the Afghan provinces under his control, and reigned under the title of Ameer. In 1839 England, commencing the series of her blunders in Afghanistan, rejected his proffers of friendship, dethroned him in order to place the unpopular Sadouzai chief, Shah Shujah, on the throne, and after numerous disasters was forced to replace Dost Mohammed. His grandson became the celebrated Ameer Abdurrahman.

When Dost Mohammed died in 1863 he left the throne to Sher Ali, whom he considered the worthiest of his seven sons. Afzal Khan, his eldest son, disputed Sher Ali's, and succeeded in seating himself on the throne. His son Abdurrahman raised levies for him in Turkestan, conquered or bribed the officers of Sher Ali, defeated Sher Ali himself, entered Cabul and proclaimed his father Ameer. An invasion of the Uzbegs recalled him to the

North, and Sher Ali took advantage of his absence to recapture Cabul. Abdurrahman, finding himself deserted, fled to Bokhara, then to Tashkend, where the Russian general Kauffmann received him hospitably, without, however, offering him any active assistance. This was in March, 1870. Abdurrahman waited in silence, biding his time. The history of his grandfather had taught him that, in an anarchical country, the turn of the strong man is bound to come sooner or later. He spent ten years at Tashkend, saving up for the decisive struggle what he could from the pension of 25,000 roubles paid him by Russia.

In the meantime the Ameer Sher Ali, alarmed by Russian aggression, had made overtures to the British Government. Finding them coolly received, he came to terms with Russia, and his refusal to receive a British envoy at Cabul brought about the second Afghan war. As the British force under Sir Frederick Roberts approached, Sher Ali fled from his capital into the northern province, where he died at Mazār-i-Sherif in February, 1879. His son, Yakub Khan, after the massacre of the British Embassy and his defeat by Sir Frederick Roberts, was sent a prisoner to India. At the first news of the fall of Sher Ali, Abdurrahman had quitted his retreat and crossed the Oxus with 3,000 Turkomans. The Afghans flocked in numbers to his standard, and the British Government agreed to recognise him as Ameer, on the understanding that he would have no relations with other foreign powers.

For twenty years he ruled the country with a strong hand. Many stories are told of his severity, which betray a grim sense of humour. At the time of the Penjdeh affair, in which some Afghan troops had been defeated by the Russians, a man was brought before the Ameer, who had been spreading the alarm that the Russians were approaching. "The Russians are approaching?" said the Ameer. "Very well, place him on the top of that tower, and give him nothing to eat till they arrive!"

The punishment fixed by Mohammedan law for theft—cutting off the hand—was so strictly enforced by Abdurrahman that travelling became comparatively safe. A celebrated brigand, Dadu, was hung up to perish at the Lataband Pass in an iron cage.

He encouraged some European workmen and engineers to reside at his court for the purpose of casting guns, &c., but strongly resisted the introduction of railways or telegraphs into the country, preferring to maintain a policy of isolation. Mr. (now Sir) Salter Pyne, whom the Ameer invited to superinted his workshops, gave a Reuter's correspondent the following graphic account of his first entry into Cabul:—

"On March 12th, 1885, I left Peshawar for Cabul, placing myself entirely in the hands of a squadron of Afghan cavalry who had been sent to act as my escort. I soon found that the soldiers considered it an insult that they had been told off to accompany a 'Feringhee.' My first night on Afghan soil was spent at Dacca, at the Afghan end of the Khyber Pass, and it was one I shall not easily forget. The Shinwaris, who were not so subjugated as they are now, burst into the village after nightfall and plundered it, and some fighting occurred in the dead of night in which several men were killed and wounded.

"As a measure of precaution I was placed by my escort in a small chamber built in the wall surrounding the town, access to which was gained by a ladder and a trapdoor. When I was once in the room the ladder was removed, and I was a prisoner with fighting going on all round. My feelings in this position may be better imagined than described, and I resolved to turn back on the following morning. I was told, however, that that was impossible, as the Ameer's order was that I was to be taken on to the capital, that a receipt had been given for me by the Afghan officials, and moreover that the Khyber was closed. There was therefore nothing for it but to proceed.

"We resumed our journey and reached Busowal. On arriving, tired out and very much troubled in mind, I went to sleep. On waking next morning the first object that met my eyes was a fakir, bound hand and foot, lying in the courtyard. I enquired what he had been doing, and was calmly told that he had made an attempt to murder me during the night. He had been caught within a couple of paces of my bed-side with a long Afghan knife with which he would have despatched me had he not been caught in the very act."

On his reaching Cabul the Ameer greeted him with a warm shake of the hand, had a chair placed for him opposite his own, and continued in conversation with him for eight hours.

The Ameer constantly visited the work-shops which Mr. Pyne established, and even filed metal and turned wood with his own hands.

Notwithstanding his intelligence and enlightenment, Abdurrahman always continued a zealous Moslem. He composed a book on the duty of Jehad (religious war against infidels) which is supposed to have had some influence in bringing about the general rising of the frontier tribes in 1897, and in 1896 he assumed the title of Zia-ul-Millat-ul-Din (Light of the nation and religion).

His reign, though marred by acts of unnecessary severity, was on the whole beneficial to Afghanistan. By his strong character and decision he hammered the tribes into cohesion, mercilessly suppressing the risings of the Ghilzais and the Hazaras. In 1895 he subdued the strange-mountain-region of Kafiristan, whose Pagan inhabitants had for centuries resisted the attacks of surrounding Mohammedanism, and had even sent to Peshawar asking for Christian missionaries to be sent to them. The Ameer forcibly converted them to Islam.

In 1895 he declined Queen Victoria's invitation to visit England on the plea of health, but sent his second son Nasrullah instead. Since his accession he had remained faithful to his agreement with the British Government, which paid him a subsidy of £120,000 per annum, afterwards increased to £180,000. Sir Alfred Lyall has graphically expressed the thoughts which may be supposed to have passed through the great Ameer's mind while debating whether to ally himself to Russia or to England:

> "Shall I stretch my right hand to the Indus that England may fill it with gold?
> Shall my left beckon aid from the Oxus? the Russian blows hot and blows cold;
> The Afghan is but grist in their mill, and the waters are moving it fast,
> Let the stone be the upper or nether, it grinds him to powder at last."

The Ameer saw that England did not want any Russian territory, whereas Russia might wish for a footing in India. He therefore allied himself to the Power which was the least likely to cross his border.

Notwithstanding his severity Abdurrahman was not a mere Eastern despot, but in some respects a father to his people. Dr. J. A. Gray, in his book, "At the Court of the Amir," informs us that if a Cabuli wished to set up in business, the Ameer would advance him a sufficient sum without demanding interest. He favoured education in the teeth of the bigotry of the mullahs who wished to confine it to acquiring a knowledge of Arabic and of the Koran, and imported teachers who had received an English education from Lahore. When he had been to the durbar at Rawal Pindi in 1885, and was returning to Cabul through Peshawar, he accepted from the Rev. W. Jukes, the missionary there, a copy of the New Testament in Pushtu. In reply, the Ameer wrote:—

"I have received your letter, and regret that I had no opportunity of seeing you. I am exceedingly sorry that during my visit to the Punjab I was unable to see more of British thought and learning, but everything has its allotted time. The copy of the Gospel which you kindly sent I receive with great reverence; although I do not consider myself bound by all that is written therein, I shall, nevertheless, treat it with that respect which is its due, as a book sent to us by God. I shall take great interest in its perusal. I shall, moreover, make extracts of all those passages that correspond with the Koran, as well as all such passages as may be interesting and striking, and shall try to act up to them. It is with great pleasure that I receive this the best of all my presents."

At the same time he never really wavered in his adherence to Islam. When the English converts to Muhammadanism at Liverpool sent him an address, he replied enthusiastically, "It is our conviction that the King of kings appointed us, as well as all the other rulers of the Moslem world, to be the guardians of the faith, ... therefore we shall do what we can for you whenever you need our assistance. We shall ever be pleased to hear about you and your congregation of new Moslems, about their welfare and the progress of Islam."

Accordingly, when his son Nasrullah visited England he brought a large sum of money with him, which he presented, as from the Ameer, to the head of the Moslem propaganda at Liverpool. The Ameer's interest in this body was probably stimulated by the fact that the first to organise the Afghan army on modern lines had been an Indian officer named Campbell, who had embraced Islam and assumed the name of General Shir Mohammed Khan.

Before his death in 1901 the Ameer had sent his sword to his eldest son, Habibullah Khan, in token that he was to be his successor. Habibullah is said to be of a nervous and capricious temperament, much influenced by the mullahs and his brother, Nasrullah Khan. That he is not a bigot, however, is evinced by the fact that he visited last year (1907), when in India, the Muhammadan College at Aligarh founded by Sir Syud Ahmad, the leader of Muhammadan Liberalism, who has always inculcated on his followers loyalty to the British Government.

At the end of 1904 Habibullah received an English embassy at Cabul under Sir Louis Dane and ratified the treaty formerly made with the late Ameer. He was, it is said, especially gratified by being recognised as an independent king and by being addressed during his recent visit to India as "Your Majesty."

Afghan Customs and Characteristics

CHAPTER II

THE characteristics of the Afghans may perhaps be best studied in the Afreedees of the Khyber Pass and the Yusufzais in British territory, who seem to be the most savage and the most civilized of them respectively. The Afreedees, located in a wild and rugged mass of mountains, not capable of cultivation, have been driven, from their earliest settlement, to seek a living by plunder and the exaction of fees upon the transit of merchandise through their territory, extorted by violence and rudely distributed among the tribe. Capable of enduring fatigue and of subsisting upon the wild roots and berries of their mountains, active, wary, and athletic, and true to each other in all that concerns a common enemy, they have successfully resisted all attempts to coerce them. It is said that Nadir Shah, the Persian conqueror of India, was thinking of subjugating them, but on being shown a handful of the wild roots on which they subsisted in time of war, gave up his project, saying that it was hopeless to attempt to subdue such a people.

Acknowledging a head in the person of their hereditary chiefs, they cling more closely than the other Pathans to the democratic institutions they have received from their forefathers. Their rude state of society is still kept together by as rude and simple a code, understood and acknowledged by each individual, every member of which considers its infringement as an act committed against his own privileges. The Chiefs, or Mullicks, are indeed the representatives of the tribe, division or family to which they respectively belong, but they possess no independent power of action, and before they can be privileged to speak in "jirgah" or council, they must have collected the wishes on the subject under consideration of the bodies they represent. When once a "jirgah" has finally determined on the course to be pursued, implicit compliance is incumbent upon the tribe under heavy penalties, and the power then devolves upon the Mullicks of enforcing those penalties upon any recusant.

The Afreedees set great store by their code of honour or Nang-i-Pukhtana, a code which teaches that an unavenged injury is their deepest shame, a blood-stained sword their proudest badge. It nevertheless serves to check immorality and to prevent the unbridled exercise of their passions. Any infringement of this code is visited with heavy penalties. The amount of fines vary in different tribes, but the following are amongst the penalties imposed by all alike:—

1. A man who murders another without cause; to be stoned to death unless he be a "tarboor" or kinsman of the murdered man, in which case he must be slain with the sword.

2. A man who refuses to go to battle; to pay a "nagah" or fine of 40 rupees, with confiscation of property and burning of his house.

3. A man who acts contrary to the decision of a "jirgah"; to suffer banishment and his house to be burnt.

4. Adultery, if suspected on strong grounds, is punished by the death of the woman first, and then of the adulterer.

5. When the relatives of a murdered man consent

before a "jirgah" to compromise the matter, a "nagah" of 360 rupees may be taken as the price of blood.

The punishment of death by stoning is another custom which points to an Israelitish origin. In the hands of an Afreedee a stone is a formidable weapon, and is that most frequently employed in their petty village frays which are generally attended with loss of life or severe maiming. The stone is also employed as a pledge of faith at the ratification of treaties. If two tribes determine to close a feud or to form an alliance, or if families or individuals similarly become reconciled and blot out the remembrance of former wrongs, vows are exchanged over a stone placed between the parties, which is thus made a witness to the contract. These truces may be permanent or for a certain number of years.

Although the Afreedees cannot boast of such costly shrines as are scattered over other parts of Afghanistan, or of any of those gigantic graves which elsewhere are held in such reverence as the resting places of ancient saints, and which, under the name of "Chihulgaz," are met with all over the plains of Peshawur and Yusufzai, yet their hills are full of sacred spots, and, perched upon the tops of mountains, hid in the clefts of rocks, placed on the roadside where a spring issues from the earth, or where a clump of trees affords unwonted shade, the rude grave is to be found of some holy man deceased adorned with white stones and pebbles, where the sick resort to be healed, and those who are bound on any enterprise, to pray; and where at times may be seen the solitary lamp kindled in gratitude by one who has slain his enemy or gathered unusual spoil. More frequent still are the piles of rough stone which in all directions mark the spot where a murdered man has fallen, and many of which are looked upon as *ziarats* or places of pilgrimage, whilst on every pathway leading through their hills or the ravines and deserts which divide them from the cultivated plains are cleared spaces, marked off by single rows of stones to serve as a place of prayer for the traveller, but which are chiefly used by robbers at their devotions. More blood is shed by the Afreedees in the pursuit of hereditary revenge than in the open affrays of villages and tribes; for the latter, though frequent, are not very sanguinary; the parties being ensconced behind rocks, or in towers, exchanging long shots and making a vast display, but continuing sometimes for two or three days before a man is killed, when the contest frequently ends. Of course there are exceptions to this when strong provocation leads to more bitter animosity and the parties fight in earnest, but it takes a great deal to draw the Afreedee from his more cautious style of warfare.

The private hereditary feuds are not confined to personal acts of violence, but comprise a long series of harassing and vexatious annoyances, such as poisoning of cattle, carrying off flocks and herds, cutting off water, and burning of crops. This species of vengeance is similar to that adopted by Samson (Judges xv.), when he drove 300 foxes, tied tail to tail, with firebrands between them, into the standing corn of the Philistines "in time of wheat harvest" to avenge himself for the insult he had received through his wife.

The system of "Boongah" may be here mentioned as adopted by the Afreedees in common with other Afghans. It is the payment of a sum of money to redeem stolen cattle, and averages one-fifth of the value of the animals. When a tribe or an individual has made a successful raid upon their neighbours a negotiation is opened either through mullahs or the people of the tribe under safe conducts, and the cattle are released on payment of

Afreedee Villages showing the Towers from which Afreedees fire at each other.

"Boongah." It is an understood point of honour that animals thus redeemed once shall not again be carried off by that tribe.

The villages of those tribes which are permanently located in the hills bordering on Peshawar are substantially built and contain two or more towers. These are square, and consist for a height of eight or ten feet of solid masses of earth and stone, upon the top of which is a room calculated to hold a dozen men, with one low doorway and loop-holed on all sides. A rope is slung from the door frame by the help of which the Afreedee scrambles up the wall, placing his feet in the crevices between the stones. Most of them have a parapet above the roof, also loop-holed, reached by a ladder from inside, where the watch is placed in time of danger. These towers are secure against assault and musketry, and the Mullicks of villages usually occupy them when driven to extremities or surrounded by many of their enemies. A curious point of Pathan chivalry is that women are allowed to take provisions to the besieged, as no Pathan will fire on a woman. One man had so many enemies on the watch for him that he is said to have remained in his tower for ten years!

Besides these towers the villages are further protected by "Sungurs," or stone entrenchments, on the hill sides around them, every path of which is known to the men; they are placed partly to cover the approaches, but chiefly to cover a line of retreat into the hills when driven before an enemy, whom they are thus enabled to hold in check until the cattle and women have gained a place of safety in some fastness beyond.

The tribes which occupy these hills only during the winter months have no villages, but dwell in caves dug out of the mountain sides in spots near to water and pasturage, the neighbouring peaks being occupied by watchers in time of war, while the crags and hollows familiar to these active mountaineers form at every hundred yards natural barriers to a pursuing enemy. In no instance are the lawless habits of the Afreedees so fully illustrated as in the Zakha Kheyl tribe recently (1908) brought to terms by Sir James Willcocks. They occupy the hills at the south entrance of the Khyber, and their principal village is that of Bazar, where the greater portion of their cattle is kept. Cultivating but little land, despising the trade in firewood, which is the chief means of subsistence in the winter to most of the other tribes, they depend wholly upon plunder.

Expertness in thieving is the sole characteristic which leads to distinction among them, and is a virtue which maidens seek in their future husbands, and mothers fondly look to for their new born babes. Every male child is consecrated, as it were, at his birth to crime; a hole is dug in the wall similar to those made by burglars, and the infant is passed backwards and forwards through it with the words "Ghal shah, ghal shah!" "Be a thief, be a thief!" Their early training in such homes and with such associations may be imagined, leading as it does to notoriety amidst a nation of robbers.

They are the principal perpetrators of the daring crimes formerly perpetrated in the Peshawar cantonments, but by no means confine themselves to these; they rob the Bangash of Kohat and the Khuleel of Peshawar on the Attock road and in the districts of the Cabul river; and no other Afreedee tribe is safe from their depredations. Their want of faith is so notorious that their oaths are not considered sufficient security even in Afreedee jirgahs which require from them hostages or some substantial pledge when it is necessary to enter into engagements with him.

Customs and Characteristics

It is said that being without a ziayarat or place of pilgrimage in their own borders, and being thus obliged to resort to the territory of their more fortunate neighbours, they seized and killed the first holy man who came in their way. The stones were heaped over him and in a few days the Zaka Kheyl were proudly paying their devotions at the grave of their own "Pir" (saint). Their little intercourse with Peshawar removes them from that control which we possess over other tribes who resort to our markets; whilst their independent bearing towards their neighbours is caused by the circumstance of the road which leads from their lower to their upper seats lying entirely in their own lands. In common with all Afghans, the Afreedees exercise a rough hospitality and offer an asylum to any fugitive endeavouring to escape from an avenger, or from the pursuit of justice; and they would undergo any punishment or suffer any injuries rather than deliver up their guest. This hospitality, for which they are notorious, is carried to such extremes as to cripple their means. An unlimited supply of beds, blankets and food is the mark of a true Afghan Mullick; one who resorts to economical arrangements in his household is lightly esteemed however excellent his character may be in other respects: so also is the Mullick who keeps food of two qualities, the superior for his own use, the inferior for that of his guests.

In every village is a place of public resort and for the entertainment of guests called the "Hoojra," which is sometimes the property of individual Mullicks, but more frequently of the village. Loose characters of the village more frequently pass the night at the "Hoojra" than in their own houses.

Closely connected with their habits of hospitality is the duty of "nanawatai" (lit. entering in), by which the refugee who claims protection, no matter who he is or what he has done, is entitled to it. This is best illustrated by a story often told on the frontier. "A debtor proceeding to Peshawar with some articles for sale met a creditor who demanded the settlement of his long overdue loan. Payment was promised after the sale of the goods now on their way to market. The creditor demanded security, but was told he must trust the word of the debtor who had nothing to give in pledge. 'Give me this as security,' said the creditor, placing his hand on the debtor's long knife stuck as usual in his girdle—a deadly insult. 'Take it' said the debtor, stabbing the other on the spot. He then fled, followed by relatives of the deceased. Approaching a tower, the pursued sought 'refuge in Allah's name.' Having inquired from the murderer whom he had killed, the chieftain of the tower replied, 'You have killed my own brother, but as you have asked refuge in God's name, in His name I give it.' Forthwith the pursued was drawn up into the tower and the pursuers sternly forbidden to approach. When they departed the chieftain then gave the refugee half an hour's grace, swearing by Allah to slay him if after that he should be seized. The refugee made good use of the half-hour and escaped for that occasion at least."

Many have been the Afghan brigands or freebooters of the Robin Hood type. Such a one was Hyder under the Sikh government, whose deeds of cunning and enterprise have rendered him famous. His power of personating other men was so successful that one of his favourite pastimes was to pass himself off as an orthodox Hindu or Sikh, and, falling into company on the road with Bunniahs (merchants) and others, jog along with them on the most friendly terms, till their arrival at a convenient ravine or hollow enabled him to throw off the mask and fall on his prey, easing conscience and expiating the curses he had been invoking upon the faithful by cutting the throats of his victims. The tendon achilles of his feet were cut by the Sikhs on his falling into their hands, but he continued to be as active as ever on horseback. Many robbers float down some river on a " Shinaz " or inflated skin till they come to the village where they wish to commit a burglary. The Michin Mohmands are particularly expert in this mode of passage; gangs of them float down a river by night and surprise a village, murdering some of the inhabitants and carrying off property and Hindoos, forcing the latter to get upon their backs while they swim across.

The chief object for which raids are committed by the Afreedees on the Peshawar cantonments is to steal rifles from the sentinel outposts, These rifles are said to be worth their weight in rupees among the hills. It is no very unusual thing to hear the sound of brisk firing going on at night on the circular road which runs round cantonments, between some sentinel post and a band of Afreedee marauders, till horrible shrieks show that some shot has told.

They are of course extremely suspicious not only of the English but of each other. A story is told of a Deputy Commissioner who wished to sow dissension in a "jirgah." He solemnly called the greybeards into his tent one by one and put to each the query " How's your parrot ? " letting him go without further remark. On his exit each was closely questioned as to what the Deputy Commissioner had said, and each believed that the other was concealing some important confidences between himself and the sahib, and all unity of action in the jirgah was paralysed.

Col. Warburton, whose mother was an Afghan princess, and who spent eighteen years in the Khyber Pass as commandant of the Khyber Rifles, tells us in his book "Eighteen years in the Khyber" that it took him years to get through this crust of suspicion, but that once he had gained their confidence he could trust them implicitly. He especially praises his Afreedee orderlies: "All proved faithful and loyal, though working against their own countrymen. They would often go out of their own accord to gather information, and frequently returned with their clothes riddled with bullet-holes. When it is remembered that they were literally carrying their lives hourly in their hands and knew the cruel, certain fate which awaited them if they were taken prisoners I do not think that I exaggerate in saying that no men better earned the Victoria Cross or the Military Order of Merit than these."

Turning now to the Yusafzais in British territory we find the same characteristics which mark the Afreedees, but somewhat modified and softened by their living under a settled government. In them we have a fair specimen of civilised Pathans. Major James, late Commissioner of Peshawar, says: "I cannot think of a people to whom they can better be compared than to the Canaanitish states in the patriarchal times. Like them they were divided into a number of small independent communities, consisting of a chief town (the original settlement) with a surrounding district and dependent villages. The chief men of these communities were their mullicks or khans who are simply patriarchal chiefs with limited powers, who appear to be nothing more than leaders in war and agents for the clan in their transactions with their neighbours."

"Such appears to have been the exact condition of the Canaanitish states in Abraham's time, though we are apt to attach more importance to them from the circumstance of their 'mullicks' being known to us as 'kings,' the literal translation of the term. Thus the sons of Jacob proposing the conditions of an alliance with Hamor, mullick of Shechem, they were well received by the latter, but he would give no final answer until he had communed with the men of the city in the gate (Genesis xxxiv.). So Abraham, in transacting about a transfer of land, deals not with the king of the Hittites but 'bowed himself to the children of Heth' (Genesis xxiii.). Throughout the sacred narrative the dealings of the Patriarchs with the Canaanitish princes and people are but as the simple occurrences of every-day life amongst the Pathan communities of Yusufzai."

"Though not always sincere, in their manners the Yusafzais observe many outward forms of courtesy towards each other and strangers which one would not expect in Afghans. The salutation 'As-salām aleikum' ('Peace be to you!'), and the reply 'wa alaikum as-salām') are always interchanged. Not to return the salām is always considered wrong, and not unfrequently taken as a personal slight, and avenged accordingly. Friends meeting after a long absence embrace, and in fervent phrases inquire of each other's welfare, never stopping to give a due reply in the midst of the counter gabblings of 'jor yai?' ('are you well?'), 'Kha jor yai?' ('are you quite well?') 'Khushal yai?' ('are you happy?'), 'Takra, kha takra yai?' ('are you strong?'), &c. Strangers passing each other on the high road exchange courtesies as each plods on his way, and 'staraey ma sha' ('don't be tired') is answered by 'Loe sha!') ('be great') or 'ma khwarega' (don't be poor'). The visitor entering a village or its hujrah is greeted with 'Har kala rasha' ('always welcome') or 'har kala osa' ('may you always abide').

"At home the Yusufzais are of a lively and merry disposition, and are very fond of music and poetry; to enjoy these they have frequent social gatherings at their village Hujras. The late professor James Darmesteter published many of their songs at Paris under the title 'Chansons des Afghans.' Their music, too, though noisy, is not without its own peculiar merits, to judge from its exciting effect on a Yusafzai audience. In all cases the professional musicians belong to a distinct class termed Dums. They are looked upon askance by the mullahs except in times of Jehad (religious war), when their songs stimulate the warriors of the Crescent. Their instruments are the nagâra or drum, the surnai or flageolet, and the rabâb or violin. Their recitations are of an epic character, generally some departed warrior of the tribe being the hero; but love songs and burlesques are also common subjects. Some of the last-named are clever and witty, and do not spare the British officials who have become noted in the country.

"The wealthier classes are much addicted to field sports, chiefly falconry and hawking. Festive gatherings are frequent either at the shrines of popular saints, or at central places where such meetings are held periodically and where people seem to come together not to buy and sell or even to quarrel but simply to make a noise and be happy. Tilting, shooting at a mark, racing, and wild music relieve the monotony; whilst the boisterous groups of children and lads to be seen at these fairs as well as in the villages, show that this happiness is not a mere holiday garb."

In Major James' Settlement Report he says: "The villages have for the most part an air of great comfort; the court-yards being large with, in most instances, a patch of vegetables or a clump of mulberries in the enclosure; the mosques and hujras are chiefly in the outskirts, with wells and groves in the vicinity. At some distance is seen a wood of thorn and tamarisk, in which are the graves of the village forefathers; an enclosing wall of stone and the votive shreds which are suspended from the overhanging tree, pointing out the "ziarat" of some saintly ancient which children pass with awe and old men with reverence. The dream of peace and comfort which the contemplation of such scenes suggests is, however, rudely dispelled by the armed ploughman who follows his cattle with a matchlock slung at his back; by the watch-tower occupied by a party of men to guard the growing crops (these are obsolete features of the Pathan villages in the plains, but still true of those in the hills); and by the heaps of stones visible in all directions, each of which marks the spot of some deed of blood. We cease indeed to be surprised at the love of home which is so marked a feature of the Afghan character; for, reared in a little world of his own, the associations of his childhood must make a more than ordinary impression on his mind; but we might expect that such spots would engender other feelings than those which lurk in the breast of the robber and the assassin."

"Amongst the Yusafzais," says Major Bellew, "the occasion of the birth of a male child is one of great rejoicing and feasting amongst the friends of the happy mother, who does not, however, partake in them till the forty days of her purification are accomplished: for during this period she is kept strictly secluded, ministered to by female friends, and made to observe the most absurdly superstitious rites before the final ablution that restores her once more to society. The birth of a female child is in no way noticed except as a misfortune."

About the eighth year, often much earlier, the boy is

admitted into the fold of the Muhammadan Church by the outward sign of circumcision. The ceremony involves some days of music, feasting, and rejoicing. After the final dinner it is customary for the guests to contribute money, according to their means, for the expenses of the entertainment.

"After circumcision the young Yusufzai is taught his creed and the ordinary forms of prayer, and is instructed in the principal tenets and observances of Islam; and this with but few exceptions is all the education he receives. At twelve or fourteen years of age he joins his father in out-door work. From this time also he is obliged to sleep away from the rest of the family, and either spends the night in the 'hujrah,' or if the season allows of it, sleeps at his father's 'khirman,' or threshing-floor."

"At twenty years of age, or thereabouts, he receives a portion of his father's land as his share of the patrimony, and seeks a wife if about to settle at home; otherwise he leaves his home and seeks a livelihood by military service in foreign countries. In the decline of life he returns to his home, resumes his share in the land, and spends the rest of his days, if old, in idle ease under the shade of his own fig-tree, and seeks to make amends for the sins of his youth by a punctual performance of the stated prayers and extra devotions at the mōsque of his forefathers. His last wishes are to be buried in the family grave in his own village cemetery. The Yusafzais are very particular on this point, and it is considered a point of honour to convey the bones or bodies of relatives dying in foreign lands or distant places to the village graveyard. If already buried in another place, the relatives travel down, however far it may be, and, exhuming the body, carry up the bones for interment in their own village burial ground."

Of course, the Yusafzais who travel abroad on military or police service have their mental horizon considerably enlarged. In the village of Tordheyr the writer met a khan, an ex-subadar, who had seen service in China under General Gordon, with whom he had been much impressed. When some Pathan soldiers returned from Uganda, they began to ask for New Testaments, having been so much struck with the improvement which had taken place there under Christian auspices. Col. Warburton relates how he took some Afreedees to Calcutta, Bombay, and Karachi, and that some time after their return home he asked one of them if he had told his friends of his experiences. "Sir," was the answer, "they don't believe a word I say: so I am silent."

We have dealt hitherto with the lighter side of Pathan life, but a truthful picture of them must have some very dark shades. Unnatural vice prevails to a terrible extent, and murders are often occasioned by it. The explosive nature of the Pathan also frequently gives rise to tragedies. On one occasion, for instance, a Pathan coming home from his day's work called to his wife to bring him milk. She was unable to attend to him just then, as she was nursing her child; upon which he seized the latter and dashed out its brains against the wall, saying her first duty was to attend to him. During the writer's stay in Peshawar a Pathan, who had been betrothed to a girl whose parents refused to give her up to him on account of her youth, collected a band of desperadoes, attacked the village by night, killing about thirteen people, and carried off the girl to the hills under the noses of the native police, who had a "chauki," or guard-house, at no great distance. According to a well-known proverb, every quarrel among them rises from one of three causes

—"*zan, zer, or zamin*," gold, ground, or women. It is fortunate that a fourth—strong drink—does not operate to further inflame the tiger latent in every Pathan. But in this matter they are loyal to the precepts of the Koran, which absolutely forbids it, though some of them take opium, chiras, and other drugs.

Though never really reconciled to British rule, they are much better off under it than formerly under that of the Sikhs. The latter nicknamed all Mussalmans "muslas," and would not allow the "Auzan," or call to prayer, to be given from the minarets of the mosques. They exacted tribute with great violence and cruelty, and the khan of one village near Peshawar held his land on condition of producing twenty Afreedee heads annually.

The two chief causes which make the Pathans dislike us, especially in the hills, is that they are not allowed to put their women to death for misconduct, as the Koran enjoins, and the continual encroachment of the railway, a branch of which now reaches as far as Jumrood, at the mouth of the Khyber Pass.

Peshawar City and Cantonment

Cabuli Gate, Peshawar City.

CHAPTER III

THE Valley of Peshawar is of an horse-shoe form lying open on the east side to the Indus: on the other sides are the Khyber, Mohmund, Swat, and Khuttak hills. It is about sixty-five miles long by fifty in breadth, and contains a population of 450,000. Intersected by the Cabul river and its tributaries, the principal of which are the Swat and the Barah, it is well watered and fertile. Canals and numberless channels, from which the water is drawn by the Persian wheel, afford irrigation in abundance.

Peshawar itself is the only city in the district and possesses little architectural effect, the principal buildings having being destroyed by the Sikhs when they captured it from the Duranis. It is surrounded by a lofty mud wall pierced by sixteen gates, each bearing a different name. Thus the gate facing in the direction of Cabul (about 120 miles off) is called the Cabuli gate, that facing towards Lahore the Lahori gate, etc. Passing through the Cabuli gate one finds oneself in the Qissa Kahani Bazaar swarming with a motly multitude. Here may be seen pilgrims to Mecca from Bokhara and other parts of Central Asia begging from shop to shop (the shops, of course, being merely open booths) the wherewithal to complete their journey. In one spot one sees a reciter with a crowd round him forming an attentive ring, while he declaims some legend out of the Muhammadan traditions, there a mullah standing on one of the ledges which projects from the shops exhorts his audience to be diligent in the duties of prayer, almsgiving, fasting, etc., and not to listen to the blandishments of the "padres" (missionaries) who would fain destroy their holy religion. Camels laden with firewood and white-eyed buffaloes are driven with resounding whacks and thumps through the thick of the throng, while, if it be the cold weather, a "tum-tum," or dog-cart, containing a party of globe-trotters will pass, while the sais running in front shouts incessantly "bach!" ("save yourself!") to obstructors. Ever and anon a prisoner goes by fettered, with a policeman holding one end of the chain, or a woman veiled in a "burqa," a white dress wrapping her from head to foot, with only a little openwork for her eyes to look through, glides mysteriously by. Mr. Spenser Wilkinson, who visited Peshawar in 1892, has graphically described the feelings of a stranger on entering the city for the first time: "There are about 80,000 natives. As soon as you are through the gate and inside the walls you are among them. Everyone looks at you. There is no staring and no rudeness, but you feel the eyes. The looks of the first half dozen men you pass as they sit in their shops, or stand in the street, give you a new and strange sensation. You straighten yourself and hold your head up with a resolve of which you are hardly conscious till afterwards, that if a knife is plunged into your back you will not flinch." (*Nineteenth Century*, October, '93).

The buildings are chiefly constructed with a framework of timber filled in with small burnt bricks; this style is adopted on account of the earthquakes which, though comparatively slight, are frequent. The roofs are flat and, being surrounded by a sort of paling, serve as a resort for the women of the higher classes when they

Main Bazaar, Peshawar City.

wish to take the air in the cool of the day, as they are seldom allowed to venture abroad. For this reason no one is allowed to build his roof higher than his neighbours' so as to be able to command these enclosures.

On an eminence to the east of the city is a building known as the Gorkhatri, a celebrated centre, first of Buddhist, and then of Hindoo pilgrims. It is first mentioned by the Chinese traveller, Fa-Hian, about 400 A.D. The Emperor Baber records a visit which he paid to it in 1519. He describes it as a mass of narrow and dark hermits' cells, which he could only enter by crawling and with torches. The ground was covered with hair of the head and beard cut off by pilgrims. During the time of the Sikh rule it was the residence of the grim General Avitabile, who ruled the district with an iron hand. It is related that once when passing through the Peshawar bazaar several shots were fired at him from the outskirts of a crowd. "Hang the nearest ten Muhammadans!" he said. This was done, and he was never fired at again. At the Gorkhatri, for fear of assassination, he used to occupy a different room every night. Under his drastic sway the Peshawar district remained comparatively quiet.

When the first missionaries went to Peshawar they built their house within this enclosure, wishing to live among the people. Afterwards they moved out of the city to the cantonment, and the Gorkhatri was occupied by lady missionaries, who subsequently built a women's hospital there. These ladies certainly deserve the epithet "heroic," for the heat of the Gorkhatri is much greater than that in cantonments, the smells around are abominable, and the noises at night often render sleep impossible. Worst of all, as they drive to and fro on their visits to *Zenanas*, they often have to endure shocking insults from the foul-mouthed Peshawaris.

The women's hospital built near the Gorkhatri is called the Connaught Hospital, after the Duchess of Connaught, who visited it in 1883. It was also visited by Lady Dufferin in 1887. In her work, "Our Viceregal Life in India," she writes: "Miss Mitcheson told me an amusing thing about her hospital. It is very difficult to get women to come into it, and they particularly fear the clean sheets. They think that if they go into them they will certainly become Christians. They are not nearly so much afraid the religious teaching she gives them will have that effect."

In the centre of the city, towering above the surrounding mosques and crowned by a golden cross stands the mission church. It owes its existence chiefly to the exertions of the Rev. T. P. Hughes, who was a missionary at Peshawar from 1865 to 1884. Previous to 1883 the native congregation worshipped in the mission school, but Mr. Hughes, rightly feeling that in such a fanatical Moslem city where mosques stood thick in every street, Christianity should also have some fitting external embodiment, spared no pains to collect the necessary funds—21,000 rupees. The church was opened December 27th, 1883, and many of the leading English officials and Muhammadan Khans, &c., were present. It is a white building in the Saracenic style, and contains a very handsome screen of wood carving (the pinjra-work for which Peshawar is famous). In the ambulatory behind this screen are white marble tablets affixed to the wall containing the names of several missionaries who have died at Peshawar. Conspicuous among these is the name of Miss Annie Norman, daughter of the late Sir Henry Norman, K.C.B., who died at the age of 27 after

Grain Market, Peshawar.

only one year's work among the women of Peshawar, and lies buried, according to her wish, in the native Christian cemetery in the city—the only European there. Other tablets commemorate the names of Dr. Pfander, who, day after day during the mutiny, used to walk down to the city from cantonments to preach to the crowds in the bazaar, and the Rev. Isidore Loewenthal, a Polish Jew, who, after his baptism, hearing that many believed the Afghans to be a portion of the lost ten tribes, came to Peshawar "to seek his brethren." He attained great proficiency in the language, and translated the New Testament into Pushtu. Unfortunately one night, after six years' residence, going inadvertently into his verandah, he was shot and fatally wounded by his Sikh "chowkidar" or watchman.

Not far from the church and facing the "Peepul mandi," or "market under the peepul tree," is the Anjuman, or mission chapel, where evangelistic services are held. It was on the steps of this chapel that the only serious attempt to kill a missionary was made in 1861, when the Rev. T. Tuting was preaching, and an Afghan raised his knife to strike him. His arm was seized by a native bystander and the attempt foiled.

Immediately under the verandah of this chapel sit Hindu money-changers cross-legged, with piles of strange-looking coins in front of them. They seem quite at their ease, but instances occur when they have been looted in broad daylight by Pathans, for whom the piled up silver proved too tempting. Over the way, under the shade of a gigantic peepul (the sacred tree of the Hindus), is a booth where all kinds of gaudy-coloured caps are exposed for sale.

The mission chapel doors being wide open during the time of service, natives come and go as they please.

Should anything like a decent audience collect and seem interested in what the missionary is saying, it is not unusual for the more zealous Moslems to come to the door and vociferate: " Niklo! Mussalmano!" (" Come out! O true believers!"). Whereupon the "true believers" generally rise as if recalled to a sense of their duty and troop out, leaving the missionary to harangue the empty benches. Occasionally, however, a sturdy individualist retains his seat in spite of warnings of becoming a "Kafir" (infidel), and may even subsequently follow the padre, disregarding cries of "charta zai?" ("where are you going?"), and perhaps eventually become a convert.

Midway between the city and the cantonment is the jail behind, whose walls rises the black cross-beam of the gallows, visible from the road. "Ghazi outrages," or cases of murder of English officers by religious fanatics, though not so frequent as formerly, are by no means extinct. These "ghazis" are often young tálibs (students) from the hills who have had their imagination inflamed by some mullah with visions of paradise and its houris. In 1896 a young officer was just putting his horse into the train at the station when he was stabbed in the back by a "ghazi" and killed. The man afterwards stated that it was in revenge for one of his relatives who had been killed by the English in a frontier expedition. In 1897 a clerk in the Deputy Commissioner's office was shot in broad daylight as he was driving through the main bazaar of the city by a "ghazi," who mistook him for the Deputy Commissioner himself. The murderer escaped through a thick crowd and was never captured. On the frontier executions take place quickly after conviction. Sometimes the bodies of "ghazis" have been burnt, as Muhammadans believe that no one who has not been buried with the due rites can enter Paradise. Cremation, therefore, deprives the "ghazi" of the honours of martyrdom.

The cantonments themselves consist of a few hundred bungalows, each standing in its own compound. Formerly, owing to the want of a proper water supply, Peshawar was so unhealthy as to receive the name of the "charnel-house across the Indus." But now matters have much improved; a large marsh near the city has been drained and trees planted between it and cantonments; a pure supply of water is obtained from the Bara river and proper sanitation introduced. The compounds are full of roses and other flowers, and present quite a luxuriant appearance in the spring. In the centre of the cantonment are the Civil Courts, round which all through the day in the winter may be seen groups of Afreedees and others squatting and waiting for decisions. They also doubtless use their opportunities of finding out weak spots in the cantonments with a view to night raids. Close by are the military hospitals, often sadly crowded. Many a young soldier arrives in Peshawar only to die of the dreaded enteric fever, for in spite of all precautions the climate remains a dangerous one. In 1892 eighty deaths occurred between August and November.

The European cemetery lies about a quarter of a mile from cantonments and has a striking effect, being a kind of green oasis in the stony plain around. It is enclosed with walls and carefully watered, and abounds with trees and flowers. In this climate funerals take place within twenty-four hours after death, and at a military funeral the coffin is brought to the cemetery on a gun carriage drawn by four horses and draped with the Union Jack. At the conclusion of the service a firing party fire three volleys in the air as a salute to their departed comrade. The band, which generally accompanies the funeral, always strikes up a brisk air as the men march back to their barracks, with the object probably of keeping up their spirits.

In the centre of the cantonments where two roads meet is the Mackeson monument in memory of Col. Mackeson, formerly Commissioner of Peshawar, who was assassinated in the verandah of his bungalow in 1853, while reading a petition presented to him by a "Gazi." Mr. Clark, the first missionary to Peshawar, has described how the mark of Col. Mackeson's blood was still visible on one of the pillars of the verandah, when he attended the first meeting held there to inaugurate the Peshawar Mission under the auspices of Col. (afterwards Sir Herbert) Edwardes, his successor. Col. Mackeson had strongly deprecated any missionaries coming to Peshawar for fear of their presence leading to disturbances, but Edwardes was heartily in sympathy with the project, and said "We are safer doing our duty than neglecting it." During the six years of his commissionership (1853-58), which covered the stormy period of the mutiny, he showed a lively interest in the mission, and often when the day's work was done would walk over to the mission house close by to refresh himself by spiritual converse with the missionaries.

The whole cantonment is surrounded by a circular road about three miles in length, outside which stretches the barren stony plain of Peshawar to the foot of the Khyber Hills, about twelve miles distant. Formerly a cordon of sentries was stationed round this road at intervals of forty yards apart. These are now replaced by guard houses each of them occupied by a small number of native or English troops. It is from these guard-houses that the rifle thefts so well known on this frontier often take place, as the Afreedee on occasion is quite willing to risk his life for a rifle. The plain outside cantonments has witnessed some strange scenes, especially during the mutiny, when some four thousand troops suspected of disaffection were disarmed, greatly to the disgust of their English officers, one of whom committed suicide in consequence. The affair was most dexterously executed by Sir Sydney Cotton, then commanding the Peshawar division. The native infantry were marched away from their fire-arms, which had been piled as if for some drill purpose, and when clear of them, the European troops with loaded arms (who were concealed behind barracks and ready for action) rushed out, seized the arms, and conveyed them under a sufficient escort to the arsenal. The Sepoys taken by surprise were utterly powerless. Finding themselves without arms they began to desert. From one regiment (the 51st Native Infantry) between two and three hundred men deserted. At their head was the Subadar Major, or senior native non-commissioned officer of the regiment. The men fled into the district, mostly making for the surrounding hills. Here was another danger of a most formidable character. The disarming of soldiers in a country like the Peshawar valley was of little use unless the utmost vigilance was adopted. The troops had only to look for arms and they would soon find them. To put a summary stop, therefore, to desertion was the first consideration. Pursuit was ordered, and the Subadar Major and one hundred and twenty of his men were captured.

He was tried by general court martial for desertion and sentenced to be hanged. The whole force in cantonment, consisting of seven or eight thousand men, armed and disarmed, horse and foot and artillery, were formed up on parade to witness the execution. A gallows was erected on the parade ground, and notice was given in the surrounding country of the approaching event.

With the Afghans

The first execution of a deserter was under all circumstances a measure of desperate uncertainty. A large body of native cavalry were present, over whom there could be no restraint whatever, if they had broken into mutiny, as there was not in the Peshawar valley at that moment one European cavalry soldier. Many thousands of Pathans from the district had flocked in to witness the execution, and it was quite impossible to say how such a matter would terminate.

The European force drawn up for action was comparatively small in number (not more than twelve hundred men, including artillery), whilst the native troops on parade amounted to nearly six thousand. Previous to the execution, Gen. Sir Sydney Cotton, with his staff, passing the several columns, which were formed up on three sides of a square, addressed the men, expressing his determination to punish mutiny and desertion severely. The execution took place without disturbance, and as affairs progressed many instances of this kind occurred, and, during the mutiny, a general parade was held every Tuesday morning at which the troops were compelled to witness rewards and punishments given and inflicted. Altogether in these months five hundred and twenty-three military executions took place on the Peshawar parade ground. Forty-four mutineers were blown from guns, twenty hanged, and four hundred and fifty-nine shot. These drastic measures produced a deep impression upon the frontier tribes, who kept quiet, saying, "Avitabile ka raj phir ho gaya" "Avitabile's rule has returned." There is little doubt that if the authorities at Peshawar had vacillated or shown the weakness which was shown at Meerut and other places, the excited Afghans would have streamed down every pass to the pillage of India. As it was the Afreedees offered their services to bring the mutineers to

Jumrood Fort, Mouth of the Khyber Pass.

order, and the mutineers of one native regiment which fled to the hills were hunted down remorselessly and killed to a man.

Since then the Peshawar plain has witnessed no execution parades, but frequent punitive expeditions have set out from Peshawar for the hills. Of these we shall speak in a future chapter.

Most visitors to Peshawar go out to see the Khyber pass and Fort Jamrud, which guards its entrance, the appearance of which has been compared to "a battleship stranded in the desert." As one approaches the enclosing mountains over the stony, treeless plain one is forcibly reminded of certain lines in Browning's "Childe Roland":—

> "For looking up aware I somehow grew
> Spite of the dusk the plain had given place
> All round to mountains—with such name to grace!
> Mere ugly heights and heaps now stol'n in view.
>
> What in the midst lay but the Tower itself,
> The round squat turret blind as the fool's heart
> Built of brown stone,"—

the last lines not inaptly describe Fort Jamrud itself. It is garrisoned by the Khyber Rifles, a regiment of Afreedee Pathans in the British Government's service. It was they who held Fort Ali Musjid, in the centre of the pass, against 10,000 of their fanatical kinsfolk in August, 1897, when, finding themselves unsupported, they surrendered.

Close to the fort is a large caravanserai, consisting of a large open quadrangle with sheds all round it for the accommodation of caravans on their way to and fro between Cabul and Peshawar. They bring down from Cabul quantities of fruit and the celebrated "posteens," coats of yellow embroidered sheepskins with the hair worn inside, which are much used in the severe winters of Peshawar by natives and English alike.

After quitting Jamrood the road winds on between savage-looking hills almost devoid of vegetation. Here and there, perched on the top of these, on the days when the Pass is open to travellers, may be seen the figures of two or three sentinels posted there for the protection of strangers passing through. In former times the Afreedees used to take toll from all travellers, but now receive an allowance from the British Government to keep the road for fifty yards on each side in a state of peace.

About ten miles up the pass we come to Fort Ali Musjid, perched on the top of a precipitous hill, standing right across the middle of the Pass. Under this hill smoke, rising apparently out of the ground, marks the presence of caves which some of the Afreedees inhabit in preference to houses as being less liable to be burnt or pillaged by their enemies. The ordinary Afreedee village consists of a few houses enclosed by a mud wall, with only one entrance and a tower at one corner, from which shots are often exchanged with some neighbouring village tower.

Here, or a little beyond, ends the Grand Trunk Road, which runs for 1,500 miles across India from Calcutta to Peshawar. Innumerable camels are constantly ascending or descending the Pass, each having a nose cord attached to the tail of the one preceding. A few miles beyond Ali Musjid is Landi Kotal, the last British outpost which, since the Afreedee rising of 1897, has been held by a detachment of the Khyber Rifles.

Fort of Ali Musjid in Khyber Pass.

The Religion of the Pathans

CHAPTER IV

AMONG the well-authenticated sayings of Mohammed is one to this effect: "My people will be divided into seventy-three sects; one only will be saved; all the rest will be damned." This has naturally caused great heart-searching among his followers. The sect which most emphatically appropriates to itself the title of orthodox is the Sunni sect (from the Arabic *sunnat*, "a way"), to which nearly all the Pathans belong. The dogma which chiefly separates them from the Shiahs is that they acknowledge the first four caliphs or successors of Mohammed—Abu-bekr, Omar, Osman, and Ali—to have lawfully assumed that title, while Shiahs like the Persians repudiate the claims of the first three, and exalt Ali almost to the level of divinity. One of the favourite expletives of the latter is "Ya Ali, madad!" ("O Ali, help!"), while the war-cry of the Sunnis is "Ai char Yaro!" ("O four Friends!"). This dispute has tinged the frequent wars of the Persians and Afghans with the *odium theologicum*.

The five pillars of Islam according to the Sunni sect are (1) bearing witness to the Unity of God; (2) Prayer; (3) Alms; (4) Fasting; (5) Pilgrimage.

(1) *Unity*.—The sonorous voice of the muezzin calling the faithful to prayer five times a day from the minarets of countless mosques always utters the cry: "I bear witness that there is one God." They tell with admiration the story of Bilal, an Abyssinian disciple of

Mohammed, who, when he was being tortured by the idolaters, and pressed to renounce Islam, would only exclaim, "Ahad! Ahad!" ("One! One!"), thereby bearing witness to the Unity.

(2) *Prayer.*—As regards Prayer, this being performed in public places might lead the casual observer to suppose that it involved more or less hypocrisy. However it may be with some, it is not so with others, as one may often observe individual Mohammedans at prayer in secluded places far away from the public thoroughfares. The different gestures to be observed at prayer, standing, bowing, placing the forehead on the ground, etc., are all rigidly prescribed and minutely observed. Any failure in their exact observance annuls the merit of the prayer. Every mosque has a well or tank close by it, as prayer must be always preceded by ablutions. In the severe winters of the frontier this presses hard on the worshipper, especially at night prayers. Prayer in the mosque is more meritorious than private prayer, and the worshipper must always turn towards Mecca. Travellers like Burton have borne witness to the impressive effect of these long lines of worshippers, rising and falling with military precision. This effect is enhanced by the sonorous quality of Arabic in which all prayers are said. Their devotions consist mostly of utterance of praise, and contain very little confession of sin. The opening prayer, which consists of the first sentences of the Koran, and corresponds in its frequency of recurrence to the Paternoster, runs as follows:—

> In the name of the merciful and compassionate God. Praise belongs to God, the Lord of the worlds, the merciful, the compassionate, the ruler of the day of judgment! Thee we serve and Thee we ask for aid. Guide us in the right path, the path of those Thou art gracious to; not of those Thou art wroth with; nor of those who err.

The last clause is supposed to refer to Mohammedans, Jews, and Christians respectively, and lends the prayer a somewhat Pharisaic tinge. According to the traditions, the number five is said to have been fixed for prayers in the following way. Mohammed, after having ascended to heaven on the magic steed Boraq and seen unutterable things, was returning earthwards. During his descent he met Moses, who inquired how many prayers he had been commanded to enjoin his people. "Fifty," said Mohammed. Then Moses said, "Verily your people will never be able to bear it, for I tried the children of Israel with fifty times a day, but they could not manage it." Then he returned to the Lord and asked for some remission. And ten prayers were taken off. Then he pleaded again, and ten more were remitted. And so on till at last they were reduced to five. Then Mohammed went to Moses, who said, "And how many prayers have you been ordered?" He replied, "Five." And Moses said, "Verily I tried the children of Israel with even five, but it did not succeed. Return to your Lord and ask for a further remission." But Mohammed said, "I have asked until I am quite ashamed, and I cannot ask again." Following the example of Moses at the bush, they always remove their shoes at prayer and keep their heads covered. After all deductions have been made on the score of hypocrisy and formality, a candid observer of Mohammedan worship can hardly fail to be impressed. Some of them at any rate doubtless bear in mind the saying of their Prophet, "Worship without the presence of the heart is valueless." A young English officer, who subsequently became a clergyman, attributed the first bent of his thoughts in a serious direction to watching the devotions of his Mohammedan servant.

(3) *Alms.*—It is significant of the intensely "legal"

character of Islam, that the two words for alms, "zakat" and "sadaqah," signify "purification" and "righteousness" respectively. It is owing to Mohammed's insistence on this duty that such crowds of beggars besiege the traveller in every Oriental city with their cry of *baksheesh!* One of the traditions illustrates the importance which Mohammed attached to this practice, "verily two women came to the Prophet, each having a bracelet of gold on her arm, and the Prophet said, "Do ye perform the alms for them?" They said, "We do not." Then the Prophet said to them, "Do you wish that God should cause you to wear hell fire in place of them?" They said, "No." Then he said, "Perform the alms for them." Alms are due on all kinds of property that are not a necessity of life or means of earning a livelihood. The mullahs or religious teachers are supported by grants of land, while the alms proper go to the support of the poor. Travellers among the Afghan villages have been struck by the absence of great poverty. No more stinging epithet can be applied by one Pathan to another than the word "shum" or "miserly." The wealth of a miser is said by them to take the shape of a huge snake which torments him after death. Great as is the stress laid on the duty of prayer, it is not acceptable if the worshipper neglects almsgiving. In some of the Traditions this duty receives a wider interpretation, *e.g.*, "Your smiling in your brother's face is alms; assisting the blind is alms."

(4) *Fasting.*—Fasting by day during the month of Ramazan is obligatory. The name of this month is derived from an Arabic root "ramz," to burn, probably because fasting is supposed to consume sin. As the Mohammedan month is lunar, the time of the fast changes, and when occurring in the hot weather is really a severe trial. Through "the long, long Indian day," under a

vertical sun, not a drop of water is allowed to cross the lips of the faithful, who accordingly are not in the sweetest of humours. In fact Ramazan is probably more remarkable for promoting quarrels than for suppressing vice. What the Pathan feels almost as much as deprivation of water is the enforced abstinence from tobacco. As soon as the sun is down they rush to the hookahs to take a mouthful of the acrid smoke, "drinking smoke," as they call it. The night is generally a time of feasting (it would be more correct to call it by a coarser name), till the daybreak enables them to distinguish between a black thread and a white. The first appearance of the new moon is the signal for the close of the fast, and sunset on the last day of Ramazan witnesses crowds of Mohammedans eagerly straining their eyes to catch the first glimpse of the thin silver crescent. Only the sick, travellers, and women nursing their children are excused the utmost rigour of the fast.

The day following the close of the fast is called "Id-ul-Fitr," or "Feast of Opening." On this, after giving alms to the poor, young and old in new and clean clothes assemble for prayers in the mosques. The rest of the day is spent in visits and congratulations. On the second day a *mela* or festival gathering is kept very much in the style of an English Bank Holiday, with the exception that no drunkenness is to be seen.

(5) *Pilgrimages.*—Most Pathans are too poor or too lukewarm to perform the great pilgrimage to Mecca. Those who do, have the right on their return to be called "Hajis" (pilgrims), and to wear a green turban. The majority content themselves with the shorter pilgrimage called "Ziyarat," which consists in visiting some saint's shrine. These shrines abound everywhere in Afghanistan and the North-West. They consist of a tomb sur-

mounted by a few sticks bearing flags or coloured pieces of rag, and have niches for holding little earthenware lamps which are kindled every Thursday evening in honour of the saint. Recourse is had to these shrines for the purpose of obtaining some cherished wish, *e.g.*, by women for the sake of having children.

An amusing story is told of the Zaka Kheyl tribe of Afridis, that they were once visited by a certain "pir" or holy man who reproached them with their ignorance and backwardness in not possessing any saint's shrine. The remedy was obvious. The holy man was forthwith dispatched, and a shrine built over him, at which to this day the tribe pay devotions. Nor is it only the ignorant who are devoted to shrines. The Amir Dost Mohammed before his death directed that his bones should be buried near the shrine of Khwajah Abdullah at Herat, in the hope that the proximity of the saint's remains might atone for the much blood he had shed. Ameer Abdurrahman in his autobiography gravely attributes his victories to the virtue of a flag which he had taken from the tomb of Khwaja Ahrar. At these shrines miracles of healing are supposed to be performed, and no rider is allowed to pass them without dismounting. All this the Wahabis, or Puritans of Islam, look upon as rank superstition. Among the Pathans, however, they are in a very small minority, the name Wahabi having as reproachful a sound as infidel among ourselves.

The Shiahs.—This sect, to which nearly all the Persians belong, is in a minority among the Afghans. They deny the claims of the first three successors of Mohammed, Abu-bekr, Omar, and Osman, to be lawful, and when they can safely do so, execrate their memory. The Shiahs have a doctrine called "takkiyah," that a man may lawfully conceal his beliefs, therefore among Sunnis they generally profess to be Sunnis. Among the Pathans the Shiahs are mostly found in the Kurram Valley to the south of Peshawar. The Hazaras, a tribe of Mongol descent in Afghanistan proper, are also Shiahs. Elphinstone, in his *Kingdom of Cabul*, narrates how one of them, having become a Sunni during his travels, was greeted on his return with the appellation "Sag!" ("O dog!") The more bigoted Shiahs on one of their festivals make three images of dough filled with honey to represent Abu-bekr, Omar, and Osman, the objects of their detestation, and stick knives into them. Puerile as these manifestations of bigotry may seem, it should be remembered that the Shiite sect which sprang up in Persia is really a protest of the Aryan against the stern monotheism which was promulgated at the sword's point by the Sunni Arabs. Especially in the extreme Shiahs, called Ali-Ilahis, or believers in the divinity of Ali, we see an attempt made to bridge the impassable gulf which orthodox Islam opens between the Creator and the creature. In the belief of some Shiahs that the death of Hussain, the son of Ali, at the battle of Kerbela was in some sort a sacrifice for the sins of his people, we see a certain approximation to the doctrine of Atonement which is ignored in the Koran.

Sufis.—The name and doctrine of the Sufis are perhaps better known in Europe than any other of the Mohammedan sects. This is probably because all the Persian poets whose names are familiar to the general reader, Hafiz, Saadi, Omar Khayyam, etc., were all deeply tinged with Sufi doctrines. It is true that it has been denied that Omar Khayyam was a Sufi, but his poems are at any rate full of Sufi phraseology. Sufiism is itself derived from three sources, the Neo-Platonism of Alexandria, the Christian hermits in the deserts, and

Indian Pantheism. The name is derived from the Arabic "suf" (wool), the Sufis wearing garments made of that material, in a similar way as the Quakers distinguish themselves by simplicity of dress. Their representation of the quest of the soul for God under the symbol of the love between the sexes is not unlike the mystical interpretation of Solomon's Song with which every Bible reader is familiar, only in the Sufi phraseology God is the Bride, not the Bridegroom. Life according to the Sufi doctrine is a pilgrimage through different stages—observance of the Law, purity, power, knowledge, the final goal being absorption in the deity. One celebrated Mohammedan mystic, Mansur Hellaj of Baghdad, was put to death for having in a state of ecstasy declared, "Ana ul Haqq" ("I am the Truth," *i.e.*, God), but his name is held in veneration by Mohammedans everywhere. Thus Abdurrahman, the Afghan poet, says:—

> "Every man who is crucified like Mansur
> After death his cross becomes a fruit-bearing tree."

This spectacle of an uncompromising Monotheism apparently giving birth to its opposite, a mystic Pantheism, is certainly strange. It is due partly to the fact above noted, the reaction of the Aryan against his Semitic conqueror, and partly to the fact that every theistic system, however apparently austere, contains in itself germs of mysticism. Thus the Koran itself, referring to the battle of Badr, in which Mohammed is said to have put his foes to rout by flinging a handful of gravel in their direction, says, "Thou didst not throw, when thou threwest, but God threw," a text frequently quoted in Sufi writings. Similarly the Koranic verse which rises to every devout Moslem's lips at times of calamity, "Verily we are from God and to Him we return," has a Sufistic tinge. Though the Afghan has a much coarser nature than the Persian, there is in him a fibre which vibrates in response to this strain.

Wahabis.—The Wahabis are the Puritans or Iconoclasts of Islam. No Ironside of Cromwell's ever glowed with more intense indignation against ecclesiastic fripperies than these reformers. Their founder was Abd-ul-Wahab, born 1691, at Nejd, in Central Arabia. His zeal was specially aroused by the prevailing saint-worship. On one occasion he heard a man who had lost a camel invoking his patron saint Saad to restore it. "And why not rather call on the God of Saad?" he cried from the house-roof. This was the signal for his promulgating his reforms. Forced to fly from his own place, he made an important convert in the person of a chief named Sa'ud, who married the reformer's daughter. Their son Abdul-aziz and grandson Sa'ud spread Wahabiism at the sword's point over a great part of the Arabian peninsula. At last in 1803 Sa'ud took Mecca, the Holy City, and every vestige of so-called idolatry, "from minaret to tobacco pipe," was destroyed. The Wahabis look upon tobacco-smoking as one of the deadly sins. Why so is not quite apparent, but Palgrave says probably because it favours social intercourse, and its prohibition served as a badge of severance for this austere sect. On the taking of Mecca a respectable lady found guilty of this "sin" was paraded on an ass through the streets with a green pipe suspended from her neck. At last the Sultan of Turkey, growing alarmed, sent Ali Pasha with a strong army and crushed the movement, but Wahabi doctrines have continued to spread in Arabia and India.

Saiyad Ahmad, a pilgrim to Mecca from Bareilly, was converted to these doctrines, and on his return to India raised the banner of reform, proclaiming a holy war or "jihad" against all infidels from the Sikhs to the Chinese. He entered Yusufzai, in the Peshawar district, in 1824, and fought several encounters with the Sikhs, at that time rulers of the country. For a while the superstitious Pathans submitted to his sway, believing he had the power of silencing guns and rendering bullets harmless. But he became unpopular by endeavouring to reform their customs, especially that of selling their daughters. A widespread plot was formed against him, and at a given signal, the kindling of a beacon-fire on the Karamar mountain in Yusufzai, nearly all his followers were slain.

He escaped across the Indus, and not long after perished in a battle with the Sikhs. His Hindustani disciples settled at Sitana in the Boneir district, which became a centre of conspiracy, especially during the Mutiny. In 1863 an English expedition was sent against them, and, after losing eight hundred and forty men at the Umbeyla Pass, burnt their villages.

At present the Wahabi propaganda is carried on by the pen instead of the sword, very much as the Nonconformist theologians of the seventeenth century succeeded the Puritan stalwarts. Wahabiism is also like Puritanism in this, that in its revolt against orthodoxy it has given a powerful impetus to freethought, *i.e.*, Mohammedan freethought. Thus instead of maintaining with the Sunnis that the Koran is uncreated, they confess it to be created. Sir Syud Ahmed, of Aligarh, one of the principal Wahabi theologians, in his commentary on the Koran, uses all his ingenuity to explain away the text, 'They neither killed him nor crucified him' (*i.e.*, Christ), knowing how absurd this sounds to an educated reader. The Anglo-Mohammedan college which he founded at Aligarh is looked upon as a nest of heretics by the orthodox Sunnis of the frontier, and an adventurous young "Talib-i-ilm," or seeker for knowledge, who leaves his native village to go there, does so at the risk of being scouted as a heretic on his return. Speaking generally, the Wahabis are more intelligent than the ordinary Mohammedans, and easier for a missionary to approach. The only mosque out of scores in Peshawar, which the writer, when a missionary there, was allowed to enter, was one belonging to that sect. On one occasion a Wahabi khan or chief of his village produced an Old Testament and asked to be shown the prophecies relating to Christ. Sir Syud Ahmed himself, by publishing commentaries on the Pentateuch, has stimulated interest in the Scriptures, which many mullahs forbid their disciples to read. Modern Wahabi theologians differ from those of half a century ago in pronouncing India to be 'dar-ul-Islam,' a land of Islam, not 'dar-ul-harb,' a land of warfare, and that consequently a jihad or religious war against the English is unlawful. On the whole, in India at any rate, Wahabiism is acting as a powerful solvent on the rigidity of Islam.

One of its offshoots is the sect of "Necharis," or believers in natural law and deniers of miracles. Free-thinkers nowadays are to be found in mosques as well as in churches. Here and there on the frontier are still followers of a strange heretic, Bayazid Ansari, whom his adherents called "Pir Raushan," the Saint of Light, and his opponents "Pir Tarik," the Saint of Darkness. He flourished towards the end of the sixteenth century. The great champion of orthodoxy at that time was Akhund Darweza, of Peshawar, whose treatise, *Makhzan-i-Pushtu*, written against Bayazid, is almost the earliest work extant in Pushtu. He commences his account of their tenets by observing "These dogs say.' Bayazid set aside the Koran and taught that God required no special observances as a means of access to Him. He gained a large following among the Afridis of the Khyber. He was defeated by the Cabul Government and thrown into prison. Ransomed soon afterwards, he settled in the Hashtnagar district, near Peshawar. After his death his son, Shaikh Umar, disinterred his bones and carried them about with him in a chest. Another son, Jalal-ud-din, captured Ghazni, and defeated the troops sent against him by the Emperor Akbar. Subsequently he was killed, and his brother, Kamal-ud-din, defeated and imprisoned. Two great rocks standing in the Indus are called Jamaliya and Kamaliya after these brothers, in allusion to the dangerous whirlpools at their base. It is difficult to know exactly what the Roshenya doctrines were, as Bayazid's works were burnt by the order of Akhund Darweza, and we only know them from his opponent's description. He seems to have preached a community of women and goods, a doctrine which we can imagine the poverty-stricken Afridis of the Khyber not slow to embrace.

The Akhund of Swat.—A modern saint of a more wholesome type is the Akhund of Swat, a mountainous district north of Peshawar. He was not a Pathan by birth, but a "Gujar," one of the agricultural class. As a boy he was remarkable for conscientiousness, and used to lead his buffalo with a rope to pasture to prevent it grazing on the crops of others. For some time he led the life of a wandering Talib-i-ilm, or seeker after knowledge. He then joined the Qadariya sect, or followers of the great saint Abdul-Qadir Gilani of Baghdad. He settled on a lonely spot near the banks of the Indus, where he built himself a camel's-thorn hut and lived on the seed of a wild grass and water, passing days and nights in religious contemplation. In the East devout poverty always leads to influence, and as the fame of his sanctity spread, numbers came to consult him from far and wide.

In 1835, when the Sikhs and Afghans were at war, the Amir Dost Mohammed invited him to join his army, then at the mouth of the Khyber Pass. This he did with his contingent of champions for the faith, but on the Amir's defeat he was obliged to flee and settled in Swat. Here his fame continually grew till he reached the rank of a "Ghaus," or highest degree of sainthood, and miracles were freely ascribed to him. He was a stickler for the old orthodoxy of Islam, and an opponent of the Wahabi reformer, Syed Ahmed of Bareilly. During the campaign of Umbeyla, however, the Akhund of Swat was borne along by the tide of popular fanaticism against the English, and was obliged to proclaim the "Jihad" or holy war against them. "O God! give the victory to the Lord of Swat!" was the cry of the Ghazis or warriors of Islam as they charged upon the British. The Akhund died soon after (1863), but his name is still one to conjure with on the frontier. In the Peshawar bazaar one may still buy broad-sheets in uncouth Pushtu rhyme, extolling him with the most extravagant eulogy. Since his death no one on the border has attained the same eminence, the Hadda mullah who incited the tribes against us in 1897 being a very minor luminary in comparison.

The Koran.—No one nowadays is likely to speak of the Koran as the first English translator, Alexander Ross, did in his preface :—

> Good reader, the great Arabian imposter now at last after a thousand years is arrived in England, and his Alcoran or Gallimaufry of Errors (a Brat as deformed as the Parent and as full of heresies as his head was of scurf) hath learned to speak English.

Great critics like Carlyle and Goethe, and great oriental scholars like Palgrave and Palmer have taught us to look upon the Koran with other eyes. Probably the sanest estimate both for and against is given by Goethe in his *West-oestlicher Divan* :—

> However often we turn to it, at first disgusting us each time afresh, it soon attracts, astounds, and in the end enforces our reverence. Its style in accordance with its contents and aim is stern, grand, terrible —ever and anon truly sublime. Thus this book will go on exercising through all ages a most potent influence.

When we add to this the incomparable rhythm of the Arabic language at its purest, and the magic potency which the Oriental has always attached to the arts of reading and writing, it is no wonder that every Mohammedan repeats exultantly the opening words of the second chapter, "This is the Book! There is no doubt in it." Critics have pointed out that the most striking passages are found in the short chapters placed near the end (though earliest in date of composition) describing the terrors of the resurrection and the Last Day: "when the children's hair grows white with anguish, and the girl who was buried alive shall ask for what sin she was slain." Here and there we have an autobiographical note which presents the Prophet in a milder aspect, "Did He not find thee an orphan and give thee shelter? And find thee erring and guide thee? And find thee poor with a family and nourish thee? Therefore oppress not the orphan." And once what looks like a wistful guess after a higher truth, "If God had a son, I should be the first to worship him." These, however, are not the passages quoted by the mullahs when confronted with a Christian disputant. Then they are never tired of declaiming the Sura-Ikhlas or Chapter of Unity which, though one of the shortest, is held to be equal in value to one-third of the Koran. "Say He is One God the Eternal: He begetteth not neither is begotten, neither is there any like to Him." This insistence on the Unity of sheer Power as contrasted with a Unity of Love is the main reason of the sterility of Islam. A striking example of the effect of, not a few words, but *three letters* of the Koran is given in the history of Mahmud of Ghazni. After his victories in India he sent a message to the Caliph of Baghdad demanding the cession of Samarcand. The Caliph refused. Whereupon Mahmud replied in a letter, "Dost thou desire that I with thousands of elephants should march against thee, overthrow thy rule, and raze to the ground all thy cities and towns and send their dust loaded on elephants to Ghazni?" All he received in answer to this was a blank sheet from the Caliph with the customary commencement, "In the name of the most merciful God," followed by the letters A.L.M. For a long time the Sultan and his courtiers puzzled over this till one remembered that the three letters commenced a chapter in the Koran called "The Chapter of the Elephant," which commemorates the destruction of the army in which were several elephants sent by Abraha, King of Yemen, against Mecca. The effect of this on Sultan Mahmoud was such that he swooned away. When he came to himself he wept and made his excuses to the envoy and sent him to the Caliph with many presents. In this instance at any rate the Koran acted as a peacemaker.

It is needless to say to what an extent the Book is venerated. Believed as it is to have superseded all previous revelations, for a time the Mohammedan world was rent asunder with the dispute whether the Koran were created or uncreated. Orthodoxy won the day, and it was settled that in its essence it is uncreated.

Copies of it are carried on the head and never below the waist. They often bear stamped on the cover, "Let none touch it but the purified," *i.e.*, it should only be handled by true believers. Before being opened it is generally kissed, and a cloth is sometimes held awning-fashion overhead lest a passing bird should defile it. It is not lawful to publish a separate translation, though an interlinear one may be permitted. It is also customary to take auguries from the Koran by opening it at random and deciding according to the text that first meets the eye.

The Traditions, or Hadis.—The word "tradition" in Mohammedan theology bears a very different meaning from that which it has in Christian. If we can imagine our Lord to have been in the habit of laying down minute regulations on all the details of daily life, and these to have been subsequently collected under different heads, such as Marriage, Fasting, Dress, &c., we should have an exact parallel to the Mohammedan "Traditions." Vast volumes of closely printed Arabic, the sifted residuum of a still vaster quantity, purport to be Mohammed's utterances on all subjects which a Mohammedan ought to know for his soul's health, from the manner of using a tooth-brush to the arrangement of the seven heavens. In the early years of Islam men like Bokhari used to devote their lives to journeying about and collecting sayings of Mohammed, examining the "isnad" or chain of authorities on which they depended, and rejecting or preserving them accordingly. The collections of traditional sayings held to be correct by the Sunnis are six in number, the Shiahs having a collection of their own. Some Mohammedan customs, such as circumcision and the wearing of beards, depend, not on the Koran, but on the traditions. The aim of the true believer is to conform exactly to the practice of the Prophet in every minute detail. Thus many dye their beards red and clip the hair of the upper lip closely because he is reported to have done so. Hatred of Europeans has been increased by the fact that he said blue eyes were enemies to Islam. Ahmed Ibn Hanbal, one of the great traditionalists, would never eat water-melons because he could not discover whether the Prophet ate them with or without the rind, or bit, broke, or cut them. Mohammed was fond of honey. If anyone says he does not like honey, he, *ipso facto*, is proved an infidel. Such is the dictum of one of the leading Pathan theologians. Some of the traditions exalt Mohammed to a superhuman degree. God is reported to have said to him, "If it had not been for thee, I would not have created the heavens and the earth." This is a saying well known and frequently repeated in every bazaar in India. Just as the Romanist has recourse to the verse investing Peter with the keys, and the Quaker to that dispensing with local worship, so Mohammedan Sufi and Obscurantist alike find weapons in the vast armoury of the Traditions. Such for the for the former are the sayings, "He who knows himself knows God," "I was a hidden treasure, and I desired to be known; therefore I created man." The bigot, on the other hand, when asked to read the Bible, quotes the Prophet's dictum, "If Moses was alive, he would have followed me." This doubtless was intended to prevent his followers consulting the Old Testament. On the occasion when Omar brought one into his presence, he is said to have turned red with anger and to have delivered himself as above. Some of the sayings have a Johnsonian or Cromwellian common-sense about them. Thus to a follower who said he had turned his camel loose and trusted God to look after it, Mohammed replied, "Tie up your camel *and* trust in God." To one of a

Hamlet-like disposition he said, "Quit the doubtful for what you are not in doubt of." Some of them betray a gross anthropomorphism, *e.g.*, "My Lord came to meet me and stretched forth His hands to greet me, and looked into my face and laid His hands between my shoulders, so that I felt the coolness of his finger-tips."

Others are merely echoes of Christ's sayings which had probably become known through the Apocryphal Gospels current in the Syrian Church. God is represented as saying at the judgment day, "O ye sons of men, I was sick and ye visited Me not," etc., quoting the whole passage from St. Matthew xxv. It is remarkable that this should have been put into Mohammed's mouth as it directly militates against the Islamic conception of God as an irresponsible despot. Other sayings of this stamp are, "God is more merciful than a mother to her child;" "One hour's justice is better than seventy years of worship." Some might furnish hints for poems, *e,g.*, "God waits till the third watch of the night; then He descends to the lowest heaven and cries 'Does any repent? Does any implore forgiveness? Does any supplicate?' till the first glimmering of dawn." Some of these Traditions have no doubt had a humanizing effect. Such as the famous "Honour the guest though he be an infidel," which has often been useful to a missionary when approaching a bigoted Pathan village. Others throw a lurid light on the darker side of Mohammed's character. Thus, when informed of the assassination of one of his enemies, and asked if it mattered, he replied, "Two goats will not knock their heads together for it." From these instances it will be seen that the Traditions have had as great a weight in determining Mohammedan law and theology as the Koran itself.

Talib-i-ilms and Mullahs.—The "Talib-i-ilm," or seeker

after knowledge, is an embryo mullah. His very title springs out of one of Mohammed's sayings, "Seek wisdom even if you have to go to China for it." After having as a boy read through the whole Koran mechanically in Arabic, which is like making an English boy read the Old Testament in Hebrew, and picked up a smattering of "mantiq" logic, sarf-i-nahw (Arabic grammar), and "fiqh" (theology), he roams about from village to village, living on charity and sitting at the feet of different mullahs. Some of them have wonderful memories and develop into "Hafizes," *i.e.*, those who know the Koran by heart. It is often customary during a religious discussion to turn to a Hafiz and ask him to repeat the passage in question, the Koran being somewhat difficult to refer to, not having its verses numbered. Many mosques depend on a "wakf" or foundation, whether of land or money, which goes to support the mullahs and "talibs." The mullahs often write charms for patients which consist of verses of the Koran, the ink to be washed off and drunk by the recipient. Popular mullahs, such as the Akhund of Swat, are freely credited with the power of working miracles. Though a Pathan may have a certain contempt for a mullah, evinced by the popular saying, "Two mullahs make a man," he is often abjectly afraid of being cursed in Arabic, the sacred language. Mullahs, if insulted or hurt, have the power to excommunicate a neighbourhood by refusing to perform burial rites, etc. In fact, though the Prophet said, "There shall be no monkery in Islam," the mullahs practically play the parts of priests and monks, especially with the ignorant, who are in the vast majority. As murders in Ireland have sometimes been caused by a priest denouncing some one from the altar, so some wild spirit, thirsting for the Mahommedan paradise promised to martyrs, will consult his mullah before setting out to kill some infidel. In the first years of English occupation of the Punjab such outrages were common. In one case a mullah who had incited a Ghazi (murderer) to attack Lieut. Edwardes, received twelve years' imprisonment, while the Ghazi was hung. On the Russian frontier the methods are more drastic, the mullah being generally hung also. Such cases still occur in Peshawar and other frontier districts, where the embers of fanaticism are always smouldering. The ordinary routine of a mullah's life consists in instructing students in the Koran and other branches of learning, conducting the five daily prayers, assisting at marriages and funerals, etc. They are not above lending money out at usury, though this is strictly forbidden in the Koran, and land is often mortgaged to them. While the lower class of mullahs are grossly ignorant, some are men of deep though limited learning, and good Persian and Arabic scholars. If a missionary chance to approach the village, the mullah is expected to do battle for the faith, as he sits in the mosque with his admiring students round him. He will commence by trying to get the missionary into some logical trap, *e.g.*, by asking if God is "muraqqab" or "basit," simple or compound. The missionary must make up his mind to be regarded as worsted in any case, and may think himself fortunate if his defeat is not emphasized by stone-throwing as he leaves the place. As a rule the mullahs will not look at the Bible, and forbid their followers to do so. Some, however, are more liberal-minded and read the Scriptures, putting their own glosses on them, *e.g.*, that "the Prince of this world" is Mohammed. They commonly use rosaries with ninety-nine beads, each representing one of the names of God. On Fridays the chief bazaar of Peshawar swarms with mullahs who come in from the villages to pay their devo-

The Principal Mosque, Peshawar.

tions in the principal mosque in the city. When two friends meet they embrace heartily, putting their heads side by side, each with his chin on the other's shoulder, and reiterating their inquiries, "Are you well? Are you very well? Are you exceedingly very well?" without stopping for an answer. Obstructive as they generally are to the spread of anything like new ideas, they at any rate sometimes range themselves on the side of civilization and humanity. Elphinstone, in his *Kingdom of Cabul*, tells us that mullahs will go with the Koran between two tribes drawn up for conflict and bring them to an agreement Charles Masson, in his travels in Afghanistan, mentions his having been robbed and stripped, and that when his captors were debating whether to make a slave of him, and appealed to their mullah, he forbade it, and ordered the restoration of his property. Mullahs themselves have been known to fall victims to the more fanatical of their followers. Thus on one occasion some Yusafzais found a mullah making a copy of the Koran. "You tell us these books come from God, and here you are making them yourself!" and struck off his head without waiting for an explanation.

Magic, Charms, the Evil Eye.—Magic is divided into two kinds, lawful and unlawful. The lawful kind, according to the Koran, was that practised by Solomon by means of the secret name of God. In virtue of this he obtained mastery of the jinns, birds, and winds. On one occasion he ordered the throne of the Queen of Sheba to be brought to Jerusalem in a moment, a miracle which resulted in the Queen's conversion from idolatry. Solomon's knowledge of the secret name seems to have been buried with him, but other names of God commonly known are believed to be efficacious in the milder kinds of enchantment. The darker side of magic is attributed to the evil jinns who listen at the doors of heaven "to steal the words of the angels." Shooting stars are believed to be missiles hurled by the angels at these diabolical eavesdroppers. What secrets they discover they whisper to the fortune-tellers. Presages of the future are sometimes formed from the position assumed by arrows poured carelessly out of a quiver, also by touching their rosaries. A favourable or unfavourable event is supposed to follow according as the bead touched is odd or even, counting from the top of the string. Belief in charms is prevalent even among the educated. The late Amir Abdurrahman mentions in his memoirs that once during a military review a soldier deliberately shot at him as he was sitting in a chair. The bullet passed through the back of the chair and wounded a page-boy standing behind. He attributes his escape entirely to a charm written on a piece of paper, which a holy man had given to him when a boy. He says:—

> "At first I did not believe in its power to protect; I therefore tried it by tying it round the neck of a sheep, and though I tried hard to shoot the animal, no bullet injured her."

If the Amir's faith in charms was of this robust texture, it may be imagined that ordinary people place implicit reliance on them. Little silver amulets containing texts of the Koran are largely used against a less substantial, but not less dreaded, danger than bullets—the Evil Eye. This superstition, which is so widely spread, is naturally rife among the superstitious Pathans. As mentioned above, one of the Traditions states that blue eyes are hostile to Islam, and therefore Europeans are generally credited with the evil eye. Sometimes, to avert its effect, they spit upon the ground when passing an Englishman, The great John Nicholson, when a native once did this in his presence, considered it an insult, and forced the unfortunate man to lick up his spittle. Race-hatred often reinforces superstition. Although the Koran expressly states that the food of Christians is lawful for Mohammedans, as they are also "People of the Book," *i.e.*, possessors of a written revelation, very few Mohammedans have the courage to eat with Europeans. In this matter they have been largely infected with Hindu ideas. The vessels out of which a European guest eats are generally broken after his departure, lest they should defile some Moslem lip.

Belief in astrology is also deep-seated. Great importance is attached to the horoscope cast at a child's birth. The great religious authority, Maulana Rumi, much revered by the Pathans, says in his *Masnavi* :—

"The man who under Venus' influence is born
Is amorous and ambitious, with greed torn ;
If Mars his planet be, his temper's bellicose,
War, scandal, litigation—these he most doth choose."
(*Redhouse's Translation.*)

Amir Abdurrahman consulted astrologers for the minutest details of life, even down to the proper time for cutting nails. When Prince Nasrullah Khan returned to Cabul from his journey to England he was kept waiting outside the city for nearly a week, though he and his father, the Amir, were longing to see each other, because the astrologers decided it was not a propitious day for them to meet. Dreams, of course, are greatly believed in, especially those in which the Prophet Mohammed himself appears. The Amir Abdurrahman asserts in his autobiography that he was taught to read by a man who appeared to him in a dream, though he was previously almost entirely illiterate. Meter Lam (*i.e.*, Lamech, the father of Noah) is said to have appeared in a dream to

Sultan Mahmud of Ghazni, and to have informed him that he was buried in the district of Lugman, in order that the Sultan might build a shrine over him, which he did. It is one of the *chhal-gazas*, or forty-feet long tombs, and is a famous centre of pilgrimage. These saints are often supposed to grow in their tombs, and one buried in the Peshawar cantonments threatened to grow quite across the road till his guardians were informed by the Commissioner that he must curb himself within the limit of nine yards, which he accordingly did. Groups of prisoners with their guards on the way from the prison to the courthouse may be often seen standing in an attitude of supplication before this Nau-gaza, or nine-yarder, and entreating the saint's intercession or help. Europeans and their customs are naturally looked upon with great suspicion by eyes like these, the Freemasons' Lodge at Peshawar being regarded as the headquarters of the Black Art. It is popularly believed that he who has his photograph taken becomes an infidel. When the Amir was about to be photographed at Rawal Pindi, one of his chief officers rushed up to the camera and covered it with both hands, believing it to be a new and very deadly kind of gun. Land surveying across the border has been attended with considerable danger, as they believe the man with the compass (theodolite) has the power of looking through walls, and even into the sacred precincts of the women's apartments. Furious attacks have sometimes been made upon land-surveying parties for this reason. The English custom of firing three volleys in the air at a military funeral excites great interest. "Do you think," said one sage to the writer, "that you can frighten away the angel of death with your guns?" Their own belief about the grave is grim enough. The dead body is not laid in it simply, but placed in a niche hollowed out on one side, which leaves the dead man room to sit up for the examination which takes place when the mourners have left the grave. This is conducted by two black angels with blue eyes, who interrogate the dead man concerning his belief in God. If the answers are satisfactory, the grave expands and becomes full of light; if not, it contracts and crushes the unfortunate occupant's sides till he shrieks. These shrieks can be heard by all animals near the grave except man. On one occasion Mohammed's mule, passing through a graveyard, and terrified by these noises, tried to throw its master, wherupon the Prophet grimly remarked to his attendants :—

> If I were not afraid that you would leave off burying the dead I would ask God to give you the power of hearing what I hear.

In conclusion, we may notice those points in the religion of the Pathans which tend to substantiate their claim to be Beni-Israel, the children of Israel. Such are the sprinkling of the blood of a sacrificed goat or sheep on the door-posts to avert danger from pestilence, confessing sins over the head of a heifer and dismissing it into the wilderness, and stoning to death for blasphemy. The first two customs are certainly peculiar to the Pathans among Mahommedans. On the whole, their religion has been fairly described as a "bastard Judaism." Many chapters in their history might be a continuation of the Book of Judges, in whose time "every man did what was right in his own eyes."

Mission Work:
Early Converts
Education

Missionary Conference at Peshawar, 1901.

CHAPTER V

GRIM and uncompromising, the mountains of Afghanistan rise abruptly from the Peshawar plain to bar the expansion of civilization and Christianity. For over fifty years a Christian mission has been established at Peshawar, but not one step across the frontier has been possible. The nearest approach to it was the establishment of a medical dispensary at Lundi Kotal, in the Khyber Pass, in charge of a native Christian, but this has since been abandoned. As long ago as 1818, William Carey at Calcutta may be said to have commenced mission-work among the Afghans by translating the Bible into Pushtoo, a translation, however, which is practically useless. In 1832, Joseph Wolff, the Jewish missionary, passed through Peshawar on his way from Cabul and Bokhara, and held discussions with the moollahs in all three cities. In 1840, during the British occupation of Cabul, some religious-minded officers made a collection of 600 rupees and sent it to Bishop Wilson, of Calcutta, towards the establishment of a mission for the Afghans. But the English authorities at Cabul, fearing an *emeute* among the people, nipped the proceedings in the bud. That there was a certain readiness to hear among the people is evinced by the fact that an officer's *munshi* (native teacher) borrowed his Testament. This was read by a moollah to his followers in a mosque, who requested to hear it again. A parcel of 200 Pushtu Testaments which had been sent to Cabul by the Calcutta Bible Society was returned by the authorities.

With the Afghans

In 1853, Colonel Mackeson, the Commissioner of Peshawar, declined to allow any missionaries to come there. Shortly after he was assassinated by a Pathan, and Col. Edwardes, his successor, gave the mission a cordial welcome, presiding himself at the opening meeting. In his speech on that occasion he said: "In this crowded city we may hear the Brahmin in his temple sound his 'sunkh' and gong; the Muezzin on his lofty minaret fill the air with the 'Azan' (call to prayer), and the Civil Government which protects them both will take upon itself the duty of protecting the Christian missionary who goes forth to preach the Gospel."

The first missionaries at Peshawar were Dr. Pfander, a noted Arabic and Persian scholar, whose controversial works are still widely read among Mohammedans, and the Rev. Robert Clark, a Cambridge wrangler. As an instance of the disturbed state of the district at that time, Mr. Clark mentions that one occasion when walking a few hundred yards outside the limit of cantonments, he met Sir John Lawrence and Sir Herbert Edwardes driving in a carriage, who ordered him to enter, and rebuked him severely for his carelessness. Now, fifty years later, the missionary can itinerate at will all over the Peshawar district. Against this must be placed the fact that Dr. Pfander seems to have been able to obtain far quieter hearings in the city as a bazaar preacher than the ordinary evangelistic preacher can obtain now. At first it was supposed that he preached by order of the Government; now, when it is understood that missionaries have no official connection with Government, it is far harder for them to obtain a patient hearing in this kind of preaching. From its first establishment converts have not been wanting to the Peshawar mission, though they have been more frequently travelling strangers than indigenous to the place. The first was Haji Yahya Bakir, who had undertaken the pilgrimage to Mecca and Medina. In the latter place he was convinced by a remarkable dream of the superiority of Christianity to Mohammedanism. He had heard of Dr. Pfander at Agra, and finally found him at Peshawar. A few days after his baptism he was found lying senseless and covered with wounds at the bottom of the mission compound. A determined attempt had been made to assassinate him, but he escaped with the loss of two fingers.

Another convert was a native policeman, Fazl-i-Haqq, of Yusufzai. On one occasion when Peshawar was placarded with notices hostile to Christianity, he tore one down and brought to the missionary at the risk of his life. He also took a dangerous journey to Kafiristan, across the border, to ascertain what prospects there were of establishing a mission in that wild region.

But the most remarkable of the early converts of the Peshawar Mission was Dilawar Khan. This man had formerly been a noted brigand, and used to waylay rich Hindoo merchants travelling on the road near Attock on the Indus. When the English annexed the Punjab, a price was set on his head. Col. Lumsden, then commanding the "Guides," met him in one of the frontier villages and offered him service in the regiment if he would give up his way of living. After some hesitation he did this, and enlisted in the "Guides." One day in the market-place of Peshawar he encountered Col. Wheler, a zealous officer who used to go down there regularly to preach. Disinclined to enter into argument, the Colonel gave him a copy of Dr. Pfander's controversial work against Mohammedanism—"The Balance of Truth." The study of it resulted in Dilawar Khan's applying for baptism. The genuineness of the change in this former brigand is evinced by the fact that, though present with his regiment at the fall of Delhi, he returned empty-handed, having conscientiously abstained from "loot." Subsequently he was sent by Government on a secret mission to Chitral. Here the mullahs recognized him as a renegade from Islam. His guides purposely misled him, and he was left to perish in the snow. His last message to the Government was that he was glad to die in their service. "The finding of one gold lump establishes the existence of a gold region though we miss the vein never so often," and one such character and career goes far in itself to justify missionary effort. The Afghans are not devoid of caustic humour, and Dilawar Khan had his full share. On one occasion when he was crossing the Indus near Attock a storm arose. The boatmen began to cry for help to some Mohammedan saints buried in the vicinity. Dilawar Khan, turning towards the Yusafzai district, began to vociferate "O Lumsden Sahib Bahadur save me!" Asked the reason of this extraordinary invocation, he pointed out that it was more sensible to invoke a living Commissioner than a dead saint.

Since Dilawar Khan's death no such striking character has appeared among the converts, and of course there have been many disappointments. Many who have begun inquiring into the truth of Christianity at Peshawar have gone elsewhere for baptism, not being able to face the storm of opposition in their native place. But there is at present working in the city a native clergyman,* the first Pathan to be ordained, who for more than twenty years has been a faithful convert. On his baptism his affianced bride was taken from him and given to his brother, a grievous insult to a high-spirited Pathan. He has learnt enough Hebrew and Greek to read the Bible in

* Now (1908) at Bannu.

The Rev. A. E. Day and Rev. Rev. H. J. Hoare with group of Native Masters and Students.

the original languages, and is a sufficiently good Arabic and Persian scholar to argue effectively with the mullahs, many of whom have come privately to him to enquire into Christianity. Once converted, the Afghans make good missionaries. being accustomed to roam long distances, and also to bear extremes of heat and cold. Mr. Robert Clark, the pioneer missionary on the frontier, used to express his hope that as the Afghans had once shown themselves capable of conquering India and had established a Pathan dynasty at Delhi, so raised to a higher power by the leaven of Christianity, they might be instrumental in effecting more spiritual conquests. Already one Afghan convert from Bannu has done good work at Bahrein on the Persian gulf. We have mentioned these cases of genuine converts first, and more might be added, as there is still a good deal of incredulity as to the existence of such.

Let us now turn to the methods employed by the missionaries. The first of these is education. There is always a great demand for this, as it is the only means of obtaining government employment. It is surprising at first sight that bigoted Mahommedans should be willing to entrust their sons to missionaries to educate, especially as the curriculum involves a daily Scripture lesson. But they have great faith in the strength of early inculcated bigotry, and as a matter of fact the Peshawar school has only produced a few converts, including the clergyman mentioned above. But of the salutary influence of the school in dissolving the rigid bonds of Mohammedan prejudice there is no doubt. The pupils, some of whom live in a hostel on the mission premises, have a genuine gratitude to their English masters, and the path of the itinerant missionary among the Peshawar villages has often been smoothed by some old pupil of the mission school who resided in the place.

In July, 1907, when seditious slanders were rife in Peshawar, the "Punjab Mission News" stated: "It has cheered one to see the earnest way in which the students have tried to allay popular prejudices. One stood up in the open bazaar to vindicate the integrity of the Government; another undertook a house-to-house visitation to restore confidence."

This year (1908) an interesting appeal was published by the Rev. H. J. Hoare, Principal of the Peshawar College and Mission School, who has worked both up to a high state of efficiency. Appealing for funds towards building a new college, he says: "The new College and Hostel will be in the closest touch with the missionaries whose work it will be. In this same garden was the old School Hostel for Pathan boys, which has had such a splendid record for the last fifty years. From this garden has gone forth a succession of upright manly boys trained under Christian influences who have been an honour to the school. In the army, the police, and in civil employ they have done well; in nearly every political agency of the frontier, where only the most trustworthy can be employed, in East Africa, Persia, Hong Kong and Pekin—there they have proved their reliability and shown that the school motto, 'Honour and Truth,' is a real one. From this hostel have gone forth the only two Afghan clergy of the Church of Christ."

Education, like other good things, has its dangers. One is that the pupil, Hindu or Muhammedan, having had his eyes opened to the baselessness of his own beliefs, should give up religious faith altogether; another, that when he returns to his native village, under fear of public opinion he should become a hypocrite and take part in prayers and ceremonies which he regards as meaningless. Such characters often pass through a prolonged stage of what they call Sufeeism, *i.e.*, regarding all religions as more or less true, and none worth being persecuted for. Having climbed on the ladder of mission education to some post in the Government service, they thenceforward look upon the missionary with kindly patronage, as a well-meaning man but rather behind the times.

Mission education certainly does a good deal to raise the moral standard, especially with regard to truth-telling and refusal to take bribes. Mr. Tyndale-Biscoe, Principal of the school at Srinagar Kashmir, says in his report for 1906, "In my first seven years here I do not remember one single case of a boy telling me the truth in face of punishment, but in the eighth year I had one boy. Then in the next year I had two instances; in the following year there were five cases, and since then the number has been increasing. As in the case of improvement in truth-speaking, so in other virtues we are going uphill with increasing speed." Successive viceroys from Lord Dalhousie to Lord Curzon, have set the stamp of their approval on mission-schools. Lord Dalhousie said, "Even in a political point of view we err in ignoring so completely as we do the agency of ministers of our own true faith in extending education among the people," and Lord Curzon personally inspected and expressed warm approval of the Educational Hostel established for young students at Allahabad. A movement is now on foot for establishing a Christian University in India, the number of Christians in the country being already as numerous as the population of Switzerland.

Mission Work: Itineration

An Ekka.

CHAPTER VI

ITINERATING work among the villages has this special interest, that it brings one into close touch with the natives. The villages near Peshawar are more bigoted than those at a greater distance. To give a clear idea of itinerating work it will perhaps be best to take the former first and then the latter.

Chamkunni. Five miles from Peshawar on the Grand Trunk Road. Visited this village in company with an Afghan convert from Bannu. It is the seat of the shrine of a famous saint, Myan Omar. Dancing at his tomb at sunrise for seven days running is said to make one a poet; a new device for scaling Parnassus. Native poets relate that the founder of the Durrani Empire, Ahmad Shah, came to this saint's mosque on his way to fight the Mahrattas at Paniput, and waited humbly outside the sacred precincts with his hands crossed upon his breast, waiting for the saint's blessing, to which his subsequent brilliant victory is attributed. We were met at the door of the native school-house by the master, unfortunately for us a bigot of the first water. He said ferociously "The Mohammedans will kill you," and on our departure incited his pupils to follow us with showers of stones. The Pathans are adepts at this mode of chastising the infidel, and a straight-flying stone from a Pathan arm may leave its mark for days. It was a relief to get beyond their range. Taught caution by this experience, on subsequent visits we went to one of the Khan's houses, who received us courteously, and brought a mullah for the purpose of discussion.

Musizai. In this village we found a mullah enquiring into Christianity, but of a very timid disposition. On one occasion he paid a long visit to the writer's bungalow and copied out a few verses from the 12th chapter of St. John, as he was afraid to be seen carrying the Testament. Subsequently he presented himself with a very lugubrious face, saying that he had been beaten. He was quite convinced of the truth of Christianity, but unable to acknowledge it.

Hazar-Khana. Here we found a Khan crippled with rheumatism. He listened patiently to the reading of the Gospel, and when he heard the verse, "Except a corn of wheat fall into the ground," etc., remarked aptly, "That means patience."

Badhber. Here the writer had rather an unpleasant experience. A Pathan of the baser sort suddenly rushed at him, and twisted his finger violently round, a favourite trick of theirs when fighting each other.

In this village on another occasion we had a more encouraging experience. As we entered it a man came up and said, "Is this saying in your books, 'The Son of Man hath not where to rest?'" This is one of the Biblical texts which has somehow found its way into Mohammedan traditions, and we were glad of the opportunity of reading him the context.

Matanni. A town close to the Kohat Pass. We had a quiet conversation with the moollahs in the village, but were pelted all the way back to the rest-house or dâk bungalow where we were staying. An umbrella put up as a defence was reduced to a wreck. Some native police looked on from a little distance impassively. They are absolutely useless on such occasions.

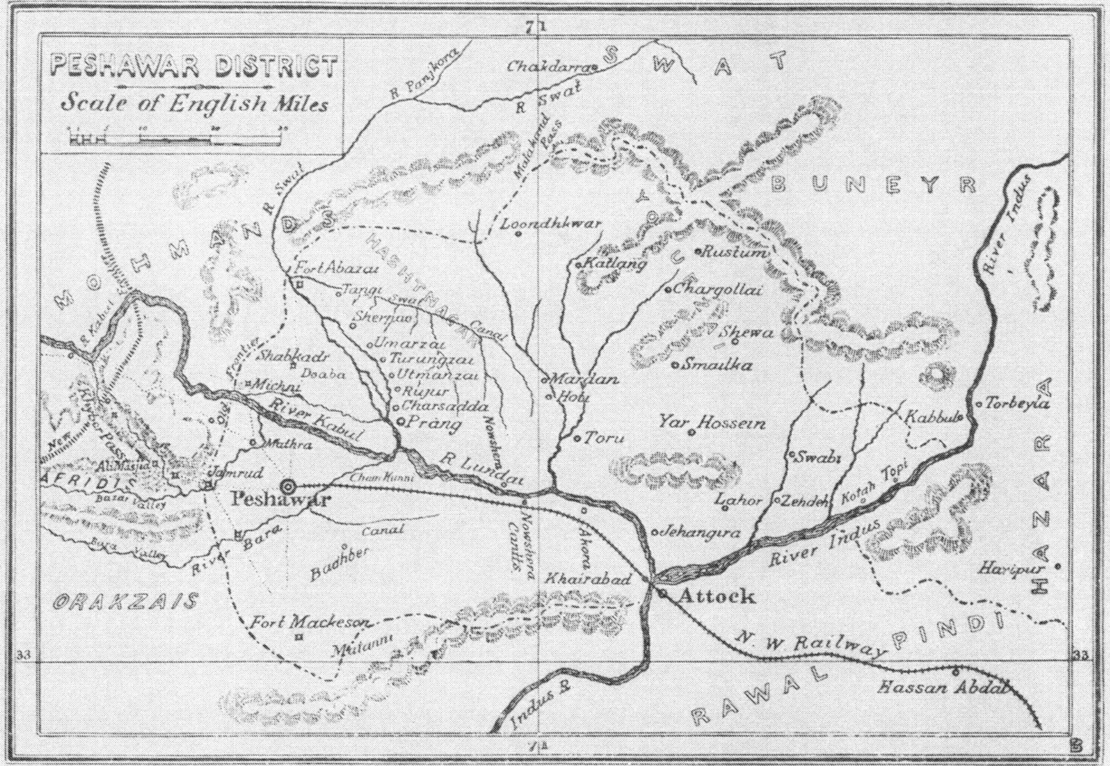
PESHAWAR DISTRICT
Scale of English Miles
SWAT
BUNEYR
HAZARA
RAWAL PINDI
MOHMANDS
AFRIDIS
ORAKZAIS
Chakdarra
R Swat
R Panjkora
Malakand Pass
Loondhkwar
Fort Abazai
Tangi
Sherpao
Umarzai
Turungzai
Utmanzai
Rujur
Charsadda
Prang
Shabkadr
Doaba
Michni
River Kabul
Mathra
Jamrud
Ali Masjid
Khyber Pass
Bazar Valley
Bara Valley
River Bara
Peshawar
Canal
Badhber
Fort Mackeson
Mulanni
Nowshera
Nowshera Cantts
R Lundai
Akora
Khairabad
Attock
Mardan
Hoti
Toru
Kallang
Rustum
Chargollai
Shewa
Smailka
Yar Hossein
Lahor
Jehangira
Zehdeh
Swabi
Kotah Topi
Kabbul
Torbeyla
River Indus
Haripur
N. W. Railway
Hassan Abdal
Indus R
71
33

Landi. A village if possible more bigoted than the last. Here we found the Khan of the village trying some murderers who sat chained together on the floor, a grim-looking group.

Taikal. Here we find an intelligent mullah willing to listen, and who even accepts an Arabic Bible. In the midst of the discussion, as we are sitting in a circle, he suddenly rises to prevent one of his disciples doing something to us. As to what that something was, we are left in pleasing uncertainty.

The native Christian Pathan, Abdul-Karim, who accompanied us to this village and told me as we left that he heard one of the villagers say "Bring a gun," presumably to close the discussion, has since been murdered in Afghanistan itself. In an access of zeal he crossed the border alone to preach, was taken before the Amir, who had him loaded with chains and conducted to Cabul. On the way he was set upon, subjected to all kinds of indignities, and finally killed (1907).

Darbangi. In a mosque we found an aged moollah who had a clear recollection of meeting Sir Alexander Burnes in the thirties. This moollah is a Wahabee, *i.e.*, an opponent of saint-worship and other superstitions, and therefore looked upon with great suspicion by mullahs of the surrounding villages. After ten visits we succeeded in inducing him to accept an Arabic Bible. If they read the Bible at all they prefer to do so in Arabic, as that is the sacred language in which the Koran is written and seems to bring them nearer the original, as in fact it does, Arabic and Hebrew being cognate languages.

Kochian. Here we found a very interesting case. A Khan of the village, who was also a mullah, and had been baptised several years ago in Bareilly. He had also been taken before the Ameer Dost Mahomed Khan, who at that time ruled in these parts. Unlike the convert just mentioned, he hid his Testament in a bush on the way, and abjured Christianity when brought into the Ameer's presence. He had a very good knowledge of the Bible, but long residence among Mohammedans without any sympathiser had reduced him to a kind of amphibious condition, *i.e.*, he conformed to some Mohammedan usages, while remaining a Christian at heart. He must, however, have made some sort of stand for Christianity, as he was looked upon with great suspicion by everyone else in the village. He would not leave the village to live among Christians as he had land there belonging to him which he wished to look after.

Fort Michni. This fort is close to the frontier, and has been the scene of more than one raid by the Mohmand tribe in the hills close by. It was here that Major Macdonald was treacherously murdered by a Pathan whom he had reprimanded for allowing his dogs to attack the Major's. Here we found a subadar or native officer in charge of the small garrison. He also acted as Imam, or prayer-leader. A havildar of an enquiring turn of mind here came and read with the missionary two chapters of St. John's Gospel.

Shabqadr. This was the scene of the fight in August, 1897, when Gen. Elles, at Peshawar, nineteen miles off, hearing the sound of firing, rode out and signally routed the Mohmunds, who had made a raid on Fort Shunkurgurh close by. Their discomfiture was completed by a brilliant cavalry charge. They had burnt the bazaar at Shunkurgurh and killed two Hindoos. This raid was punished by an expedition into their country, which burnt several of their villages. Here also a murderous Ghazi outrage took place in 1901, when a native shot two officers one morning as they were going out of the fort.

Mission Work: Itineration

Abazai Fort. Another frontier fort on the banks of the Swat river, reached by crossing on a large ferry boat. A number of native workmen who were here employed in the construction of a canal were attacked one night by the hillmen and some were killed. These canals are one of the greatest boons the English Government has bestowed upon the country, making what was before a barren waste fertile with irrigation. Here one may see the shepherd driving his flock with a gun slung across his back, in case someone with whom he has a blood feud should suddenly attack him.

A Pathan from this village went to Bunnoo on the frontier, and coming under Christian instruction was baptised. Some time afterwards, while sitting in his house, he was shot dead from outside. The reason was not definitely known.

Tangi, the largest town in the district with 4,000 inhabitants. Here we put up at the Thana or police station, situated on a high piece of ground. These police, as mentioned above, leave much to be desired on the score of efficacy. Not long ago a noted freebooter from over the frontier, with the picturesque name of Tor Lala (Black-and-Red), was affianced to a girl in one of the villages in English territory. Her parents, however, delayed giving her up to him on the plea of her youth. Whereupon one night this worthy, with a band of ruffians, attacked the village, killing about thirteen persons and carrying off the girl almost under the noses of the Tungi police. We heard that he himself had been killed by an enemy some time after.

Umurzai.—The people of this place were very noisy and disinclined to listen. In the vast cemetery stretching for miles along the road we saw a solitary veiled figure, swaying to and fro as if in a paroxysm of grief. On approaching we found it was only an enthusiastic student of Arabic grammar, who seemed to find the neighbourhood of the dead conducive to study. He accepted a Pushtu gospel. These portions of Scripture are generally safe from destruction, as the Mohammedans revere any paper or book containing the name of God. In Umurzai itself, a pugnacious Pathan insisted that the missionary had a "but" or image of an idol tattooed upon his chest, and challenged him to expose it, which challenge was naturally declined. Seeing English soldiers having their arms and chests copiously tattooed with strange devices, they seize upon this as a ground for accusing us of idolatrous tendencies!

Charsudda.—In this large village we came across a Wahabee Khan who had written a treatise in Pushtoo verse on "the rights of children," urging that they should be taught something beyond the stereotyped curriculum of learning the Koran in Arabic without understanding it, with a smattering of Arabic grammar. He has sent his own son to the mission school at Peshawar. This was the man, as mentioned in a previous chapter, who brought a Hindustani Bible and requested to be shown prophecies relating to Christ. But in spite of his open-mindedness he still dyes his beard red in imitation of the Prophet.

Agra.—Here a moollah in a mosque read aloud the Sermon on the Mount till he came to the words "They shall be called the children of God," when he handed it back to the missionary with a smile of contempt. Their minds are so accustomed to the deadly literal interpretation of such phrases which they regard as blasphemous, that they simply cannot grasp the spiritual meaning. This is where Sufi influence comes in usefully, the Persian mind being much more subtle and nimble than the Pathan.

Mission Work: Itineration

Akarpura.—After holding a conversation in this village the writer was followed by a Pathan, who demanded his watch-chain, which had taken his fancy. The request was of course refused. He followed steadily behind and was joined by another. One said to the other, "Are you afraid?" As we had entered a stretch of country in which there was no village for about two miles the situation was not exactly pleasant. After having in vain tried to wrench away the short whip which the writer always carried to keep off the wild dogs which infest every village, the would-be-thief slunk off as we neared the next one.

Yusufzai district.—This is a district farther off from Peshawar than the last one. It is bounded on the south by the river Indus, which the Pathans call Aba Seen—Father Indus. Here many interesting Buddhist remains are found, Buddhism having formerly been paramount in these regions from which it has entirely vanished. The natives look upon the zeal with which some "sahibs" hunt up these relics as one of these English vagaries for which there is no accounting. This district was also the scene of many fierce battles between the Sikhs and Pathans, in which the latter were generally worsted. The Yusufzais are the most intelligent of the Pathan tribes, and the Khans in the villages are friendly and hospitable. Many of them are retired native officers, and have seen service in Egypt and China, and consequently have a larger mental horizon than their followers.

Zeydah. In this village the Khan has actually built a roomy bungalow to accommodate English travellers. One of his sons educated in the mission school has obtained high rank (for a native) in the India Civil Service, and is a judge. He informed me on arrival that I need not dress for dinner, a strange remark to hear in this remote village. His small library contained copies of the Bible in Arabic, Persian, Hindustani, and Pushtu placed there by a former missionary. It also contained one or two volumes of the unexpurgated edition of Sir Richard Burton's "Arabian Nights," given by another English friend, and it is to be feared more diligently read than the former gift. As Khan of the village he takes part in the mosque prayers, though as he informed me, his private beliefs were Agnostic. In this village a small farmer had previously been converted to Christianity, and had undergone much persecution. On one occasion his wife was hidden from him in order to induce him to repeat the "Kalima" or Mohammedan creed. He is dead, and his sons, sad to say, have all gone back to Mohammedanism. At the present time it is almost impossible for a Christian, as such, to live alone in a frontier village. The deprivation of the use of the village well is the mildest feature of the persecution they would have to undergo. This fact partly accounts for the slow spread of Christianity on the frontier. The native Christians mostly live in Mission compounds, and therefore their influence cannot be widely diffused.

Kotha. Here we find another curious case, an old mission-school boy who has been baptized twice, once by Protestants, and once by Roman Catholics, and now lives outwardly as a Mohammedan. He assured me that he was a Christian at heart, but found it impossible to give up his land, which he would have to do if he left his village. He was very well read, and quoted to me a striking verse of the Masnavi:—

> "I extracted the marrow from the Koran,
> And cast the bone to the dogs."

Topi. This is a village close to the border and overlooked by the mountains. Hither my Pathan friend accompanied me, hiding a pistol in the voluminous folds of his garments, as he said it might be required. Fortunately, however, it was not, though we had a somewhat stormy discussion with a moollah which ended by his asseverating in a loud voice "I testify that Mohammed is the prophet of God!" Their favourite way of closing a discussion which is unpalatable is to repeat the "Kalima" "There is no God but God, and Mohammed is the Apostle of God." This is instantly taken up and repeated in a crescendo chorus by their followers so as effectually to drown the voice of the missionary. Another method is to give the "Azan" or call to prayer. As soon as the sonorous Arabic vibrates through the air, every devout Mohammedan is silent, and the missionary perforce must be silent too. Sometimes they will go so far as to pray with uplifted hands for the missionary's conversion to Islam, which is slightly embarassing. A former missionary who itinerated much in this district and had many friends among the Khans, on his retirement was firmly believed to have become a Mohammedan.

Baja. Here we found a "dum" or native poet, as anxious as any minor versifier in England to have his productions listened to. These "dums" are the ballad-makers of the frontier, and celebrate the battles between the frontier tribes and the English, somewhat in the style of Chevy Chase. Here is a specimen from the account of the Umbeyla campaign on the Boneyr frontier, when the English suffered some reverses:—

"Rifle-bullets rained as fine rain." The Deputy Commissioner said to the Commissioner: "They have with them a powerful Fakir*, against whom there is no fighting. The regiments of the White cried aloud on

* The Akhund of Swat: v. chapter iv.

account of the Pir (saint), 'When shall we be delivered? They storm our ramparts; we cannot stop the Ghazis; the sword leaves no trace upon them.'" (Darmesteter's translation.)

These patriotic ballads sound like an uncouth echo of Deborah's song in their savage exultation.

The readiness of the people to listen to recitations has been turned to account by one of our Pathan catechists with a vein for poetry, who has composed a very readable little collection of Pushtu Christian verse. The Pilgrim's Progress has been translated into Pushtu, but is not so popular as might be expected. Simple as it is, a degree of intelligence above that of the ordinary Yusufzai villager is required to understand it.

Kalabut. Here we were encouraged by hearing at night through a thin wooden partition the Khan repeating and explaining to his followers what we had said to him the evening before. As may be imagined Scripture facts are considerably distorted when refracted from one Pathan brain to another. Thus they obstinately believe that the *English* tried to kill Christ, and that God took him up alive to heaven before He could be crucified. The assertion of Christ's Divinity and Crucifixion is generally met by exclamations of "Tauba! Tauba!" "Repent! Repent!" (of such a falsehood!) It is curious how an old Gnostic heresy embodied in the Koran, that Judas was crucified instead of Christ is obstinately rooted in the Pathan mind.

A long march of twelve miles across barren and unirrigated ground brings us to Kaloo Khan. A peculiar feature of the Yusufzai landscape is found in isolated hills starting up from the middle of the plain. One little group is called the "Five Saints," another, Karamar, 3,000 feet high, is crowned by a *ziyarat* or saint's shrine.

My munshi informed me that two tribes in Boneyr, when finding time hang heavy on their hands, quarrel vigorously about the relative heights of two contiguous hills "Ilm" and "Sara." At Kaloo Khan we met the father of a young Pathan who had made the pilgrimage to Mecca and then gone on to Jerusalem. Here he came under Christian influence and was eventually baptized, unfortunately, however, dying soon afterwards. His father did not seem very grieved at his son's apostacy from Islam, and received a Bible which his son had left behind him.

Toru.—In this place we met a redoubtable opponent, a Pathan moollah who had been a "madarris" or teacher in a mosque at Delhi. He was an able Arabic scholar and carried an Arabic New Testament with him. In the early morning after our arrival we found him seated in a large circle of about 60 Pathans, ready for the fray. He turned to 15th and 16th chapters of St. John, and insisted that the Comforter there spoken of was Muhammed. This is a favourite argument of theirs, and probably due to the fact that in some ancient Greek copy the term περικλύτος ("Praised") was used instead of παρακλήτος ("The Advocate"). The translation of the former term in Arabic is "Ahmed," another form of the name Mohammed, who accordingly is supposed to be indicated in this passage. The discussion was friendly, and neither in this village nor any other in Yusafzai was violence resorted to as in those of the Peshawar district.

Hoti Mardan.—The Khan of this place was a great friend of the missionary before referred to. While we were sitting in his courtyard bags of rupees were brought in by his accountants, and eyed hungrily by the moollahs who, in many cases, are the Khan's parasites. The stricter moollahs anathematize him, as he is deeply infected with Sufi doctrines. We found in his possession the Akbar-nama or history of the great Moghul Emperor Akbar, who, as Tennyson describes, tried to construct a syncretic religion out of the warring sects of his time, and by doing so incurred the imputation, and perhaps deservedly, of apostacy from Islam. Our friend seemed to have taken the emperor as his model and to be a small Akbar in his way. During the frontier troubles of 1897 he gave the Government a large money contribution towards carrying on their campaign.

This Khan has since addressed a letter to the director of the Central Asian Mission urging that a lady missionary should be sent to Mardan to work in the Zenanas. A lady from Denmark arrived in 1904, and is now working there.

Mardan is the headquarters of the famous Guide Corps to which the convert Dilawar Khan belonged. Many of this corps died in the defence of the Residency at Cabul during the Afghan War, and their devotion is commemorated by a stately memorial arch.

Nowshera.—The mullah of a small village Manki near here has acquired a great reputation by having broken in an access of iconoclastic zeal a small black stone (probably an aerolite) which had been fixed in a saint's shrine, and to which the faithful paid, in his opinion, idolatrous devotion. He then set up as a reformer and sent his disciples armed with leathern thongs to scourge the lukewarm to their prayers. All this was borne patiently, as what might be expected from a saint, but when he proceeded to forbid smoking the huqqah, a solemn conclave of moollahs, was held, in which it was decided that tobacco could not be unlawful, as it had not been invented in the Prophet's time. Since then his influence has somewhat waned, but he acquired notoriety at the time of the frontier disturbances by praying for the defeat of the English. Another leader who has acquired great influence among some of the younger Pathans is Gulam Ahmed of Qadian, a village in the Panjab. This man gives out that he is a reincarnation of Christ. He is, of course, scouted as a dangerous heretic by the orthodox Sunnis, but counts his followers by the thousand. He has become aware of the results of the Higher Criticism in Europe as set forth by Cheyné, Driver, and others, and has indoctrinated his followers with them. This, of course, immensely increases the difficulty of missionary work among them.

In several of the villages above mentioned the writer was allowed to sit on the straw-littered floor of the mosque after removing his boots, face to face with the chief mullah and surrounded in some cases by quite a crowd of Mohammedans. It was interesting to find in one mosque, on visiting it after a considerable interval, copies of the Scripture which had been formerly given, carefully preserved. The more bigoted mullahs will tear up Testaments, but many shrink from doing so as they contain the name of God. In more than one case, when the writer's stock was exhausted, a moollah has walked with him to the rest-house, where he was staying to procure one. More than once in the mosques he has been allowed to read the account of the Crucifixion or a parable with very little interruption. The parables have been translated into Pushtu verse by Mullah Ahmed of Tangi under Mr. Hughes' direction, and are very popular.

Preaching across the Frontier

CHAPTER VII

IN the early seventies Mr. E. C. Johnson, an independent missionary, formerly an officer in the Bengal army, crossed the Frontier. He fortunately lived to record his experiences, and his narrative runs as follows:—

"About the first of March I left Rawul Pindi dressed in my usual Pathan dress and arrived in Peshawar about noon of the third day. There my old Pathan servant met my gaze. I made a signal to him. He kept quiet, but followed me. I told him I was going to cross the Frontier alone. He seemed to be deeply moved and excited at this. He said to me, 'It is impossible for you to go over the Frontier alone, for a man was killed only yesterday outside Muttra Thana.' He said he was trying to make other arrangements for me to go with a kafilah (caravan) without telling them my whereabouts. He brought to me on Sunday night a kafilah master. I told him I was a Christian faqir and that I was prepared to give away my head, but not my religion, and if he could take me, well and good. He said my being a faqir would not be known, and he accordingly consented to take me.

"After leaving the city the caravan proceeded to Muttra Thana, and there stopped for the night. My servant signalled to me not to go into the village, and he took me to a dry ditch outside. As soon as it was dark I slipped in amongst the mules and got down by the side of my Kafilah master. The police officer's tent was within a few yards of me.

"On the morrow before daylight the kafilah started. My servant took my hand and put it into the kafilah master's and said, 'He is now committed to your charge.' As we neared the frontier the gloomy hills and the noise of the crowd that accompanied the kafilah made a great impression on me. Towards dawn we crossed the frontier and reached the ferry of the Cabul river. We found the ferry crowded with the hill people. I shrunk a little from this at first, but felt that the word was 'Forward,' and that there was no going back now.

"In order to avoid suspicion before getting in the ferry, I sat down at the edge of the river and began to wash my mouth and teeth like a native. If anyone looked at me suspiciously I returned the look by looking them straight in the face, and then got into the boat and sat down. We then crossed the river. The kafilah master told me to go apart quietly and sit by myself. I was soon accosted by one of the ferrymen who demanded my fare. I told him my kafilah master would give it. He said 'The kafilah master is not giving it.' I took out a rupee and offered it to the man, asking him for change. He said, 'If you want change, come to the ferry,' so I let the rupee go.

"We then began to ascend the hills where there is no road, but only a footpath steep and precipitous. The ferocious countenances of those we met, all armed, convinced me that I had left British territory for the land of the Yagis (rebels). I looked at everyone who looked at me suspiciously in the face. To the Pathan salutation, 'Staraey masha' ('May you not be tired') I returned the proper 'Ma khwaregi' ('May you not be poor'). My guide and I then passed quietly up the hill.

"Shortly after getting into the hills a man passed rapidly by without looking at us, armed with a pistol and dagger. My guide at once said 'That is a spy; his mouth must be stopped.' Just then we arrived at a village where they were digging a grave. To my horror I found the spy sitting down with the villagers talking as we passed. They called out in fierce tones 'Get down!' I prepared to dismount from my mule. My guide, however, said something which I did not understand, and we passed on.

"In about an hour we arrived at the end of the first stage, two fortified villages in the hills. The blood-thirsty looks of some of these villagers convinced me I could expect no mercy at their hands if identified. My guide then went to stop the mouth of the spy who had followed us all the way. He offered him ten rupees, but he refused to take a pice less than twenty. I had to comply with his extortionate demand.

"The next morning we started. Just before starting a man in the kafilah asked me who I was, whether I was from Bokhara or Cabul. I replied, 'I am a Christian faqir; I live on the banks of the Indus near Mari' (which is quite true). A Mussalman faqir here saved me by breaking in 'I suppose he is somewhere from Hydrabad." I remained quite silent. We then started. The road lay along a precipitous route, and we descended into a deep valley, but before descending were stopped by armed men at the first place where they take toll. We descended to the river. The guide told me there was great danger here, and to be very careful. I got into the boat, and while in the boat a Pathan muttered in a low tone, 'That is a Feringhee.' A mussalman faqir from British territory seated behind me quickly replied, 'Do you not see he is a Kashgar man? Why do you call him a Feringhee?' I remained silent.

"Ascending the valley on the other side of the river, we found to our dismay that the spy was still following the kafilah. When we ascended the hill we found a wide pass opening out into a fertile plain on the other side. Here we began to meet many armed travellers, and I felt that my life hung on a thread. Some had been to cut grass, with their muskets on their shoulders. A heavy rain compelled the villagers to remain indoors, and enabled me to throw a large blanket over my head, thus concealing my features.

"We shortly reached the end of the second munzil or stage, a fortified village where Bahram Khan spent his first night after murdering Major Macdonald near Michni. The rain still continuing, I was stuffed away by my guide in the corner of an unoccupied house. I made tea and gave a cup to a Mussalman faqir going to Bokhara. He seemed thankful and said 'Thank you, mullah." At this village the spy again made an extortionate demand from my guide, which had to be complied with.

"The next morning the caravan was joined by Ghazni and Cabul Pathans on their way home. We then arrived at the outer mouth of the pass, where toll is again taken. The guide said, 'If we escape here we are comparatively safe, for the spy will leave us here as we are near Sher Ali Khan's territory.' Just at this moment another spy came forward to examine me, but the spy who was in my secret seeing him approach me, making an excuse, called him away. The toll was paid; each traveller as he passed was scrutinized by a noisy, squabbling crowd of Pathans. Just as my mule came up, something seemed to attract their attention another way. Taking advantage of the moment I gave a jerk to the bridle and passed through. I was comparatively safe. The great danger was now past, as all spies from the frontier left us at this point.

"We now passed along the bank of the river near the

Khyber Pass into the beautiful and fertile plains of Lalpura. The next day we arrived at Bassowul, where there is an outstation of Sher Ali Khan's cavalry, consisting of a corporal and two sowars. While I was seated among the mule bags in the serai (inn) a Rissaldar came up to me and asked me who I was and whence I had come. I replied that I was a Christian faqir from the banks of the Indus, and that I was going to Kafiristan. He said, 'I know you are from the cantonment at Peshawar.' This man would not give up his inquiry but collected others about me. They all began questioning me. I said, 'I must tell you the truth even if I have to die for it. I am not a Mussalman, I am a Christian.' No sooner had I uttered the words 'I am not a Mussalman' than they all shrank from me as from an unclean animal. The Afghan said to me, 'I know you by your eyes, you Feringhee Kafir.' An old and respectable man, evidently the chief of the village, said to me very kindly, 'You need not fear; no one will kill you here in Sher Ali Khan's territory.' The corporal also said, 'All are allowed to pass here, Kafirs, everyone.'

"The people of the caravan were in a great state of excitement, and said, 'If this had been known in the hills, we should have been cut to pieces.' They joked much with my guide on his cleverness in bringing me through, and said, 'We must watch him closely at night, or the Pathans from the hills will kill him.'

"The villagers, now hearing a Feringhee had come, began to assemble. I opened my box of medicines and began to dress the wound of a man who had been cut over the eye. They seemed favourably impressed with me, and told me no one would harm me. My friends in the caravan at night placed me between the wall and sacks piled up, and one slept at my head and one at my feet.

"The next day was Sunday. The women of the caravan gathered about me and implored me to keep well up in the kafilah, for if I lagged behind I should be murdered. We shortly reached the end of the fifth munzil. It being Sunday, as soon as the caravan stopped I went aside to pray. When I returned the Ghazni Pathan asked me if I had been to say my prayers. He then asked me questions about our religion. I took the Pushtu translation of the English Prayer-book, and explained some of the principles of our religion to him. He then said to me, after a pause, 'You people say that Jesus is the Son of God?' After a moment's pause I replied 'Yes,' and then began to explain that Jesus was born by the Holy Ghost. They began to get excited, and one fierce-looking Pathan said, 'For this word (*i.e.*, the phrase 'Son of God' which they regard as rank blasphemy) they are accustomed to kill.' I replied, 'I am ready for death.' The village people seemed kindly disposed, and wished to make my acquaintance, but the caravan people would not let them.

"The next day we reached Jelalabad. The great snow-clad hill which separates Afghanistan and Kafiristan was close in sight, and two days would have taken me into Kafiristan. I hoped to leave Jelalabad quietly and go on to the hills, but soon a crowd of fine-looking young Pathans entered the Serai where I was and, sitting down before me, asked me who I was. One handsome young man, looking me in the face, uttered the word 'Dushman' (enemy). I said, 'I am not an enemy. I am a Christian.' One then, armed with a dagger and a pistol, deliberately stepped over to my side and, drawing his dagger, lifted it above me as if about to plunge it into my breast. I thought my hour was come and said, 'Don't kill me!' Another Pathan came to him and said, 'Do not frighten him; put away your dagger,' while the one who had called me 'dushman' said, 'We don't kill here.

"In the meantime news reached the commandant that a Feringhee had come. Soon a colonel and several other officers came to me; they spoke to me roughly but kindly, and all seemed anxious to assure me I was safe in Sher Ali Khan's territory. I was placed under charge of the Kotwal (police superintendent). Many came to gaze upon me, and I was a gazing stock all the time I was in Jelalabad. The next day the Khan of Jelalabad sent the Kotwal and two soldiers to bring me into his presence. He was seated on a divan with several of his officers. He told me very kindly to sit down, and asked me what was my wish. I told him I was a Christian, showed him my Bible, said I could not give up my religion, that I wished to proceed to Kafiristan or Cabul city, and that I asked protection from Sher Ali Khan. They then examined the translation of the Pushtu prayer-book, and asked me to repeat some of the prayers. They then asked me to sing some of the hymns at the end of the book, I sang the Pushtu bhajan (hymn), 'One there is above all others.' The whole court were quite still, and listened with profound attention.

"A great stir was now heard in the court and General Gulam Haidar made his appearance. He said to me much astonished, 'How did you manage to come here?' Shamil Khan, governor of Jelalabad, said 'This is putting the head in the hand (*i.e.*, risking it) for Hazrat Isa (Jesus the Prophet).' The General looked at my English Bible, and I was told again to sing the same bhajan as before. The General told an officer to put two soldiers over me to watch me night and day. Shamil Khan told me I must wait here for about five days, till the will of the Ameer should be known.

Shortly after the Kotwal with two soldiers came to conduct me back to my room in the Serai, which I found now made comfortable for me, a great contrast to the miserable places I had to put up in for the last five days. Having heard that I had medicine, people began to flock to me from all sides. With some I had, though with great difficulty, an opportunity of speaking a word. At last I hit on a plan. When I gave a packet of medicine, I folded up and gave with it a Pushtu text of Scripture on a card.

"In the quiet of the evening, as I was seated near the fire, a Candahari Pathan soldier came and talked a long time with me, and asked me about our religion. I told him as well as I could in Pushtu the story of the Cross. He then asked me 'What do you say about Isa?' I said 'I believe He is God.' He seemed thoughtful and said on going out, 'Be careful, and do not talk to anyone in Jelalabad as you have talked to me to-night.'

"I spent five days in Jelalabad, people either coming to look at me or for medicines. With the medicines I gave away Pushtu texts written on cards. I had some interesting conversation with the Kotwal and others. On Saturday evening my guard of two young Afghan soldiers, who had been great companions to me, were changed for a rough and bigoted Parseeban soldier. He seemed horrified at having to keep guard over a Kafir. He said, 'Become a Mussalman.' 'I cannot leave Isa,' I replied. At the very mention of the name 'Isa' he drew back astonished, not knowing what to make of me. At about eight o'clock at night my friend the Kotwal came and told me to be ready to start before dawn, that, if possible, we might get out of the city without anyone knowing it, and said that the Ameer of Cabul had sent for me. That night five armed men besides my guard passed the night with me.

"Before dawn the Kotwal came, and going out at the Serai gate, I found a horse and two mounted men waiting for me. I was mounted on one horse, and with one sowar in front and one behind, I went out of the city. A short distance out we were joined by another sowar, and a little further on by the Governor of Jelalabad himself. The day began to break, and I began to see to my great great surprise that we were going back the way I had come. I asked the Kotwal why he had said that I was to be taken to Cabul, He said, 'The sentry over you was a "haram-zada" (base-born), and I did not want him to know which way we were going.'

"On arriving at the outskirts of the Ameer's territory, the governor told me that if anyone questioned me I must say I was a mullah. I said 'A Christian mullah?' He said, 'Don't speak to anyone until I hand you over to the Khan of Lalpura.' On arriving at Lalpura some of the more respectable mullahs evidently recognised me, but did not say a word to me. One of them said to the governor 'You have brought a mullah with you.' 'Yes,' he said, 'a mullah from Bokhara.' I felt grieved at this and inclined to deny it in the presence of them all; prudence, however, suggested thet I had better speak to the governor about it afterwards.

"The place now began to fill with armed men. Shortly after the Khan of Lalpura himself made an appearance. He has a most intelligent countenance and high forehead, and is very fair. After the usual salutations were exchanged, the Khan of Jelalabad called the Khan of Lalpura aside quietly, and I was left alone with one soldier in the midst of the armed retainers of the Khan. All eyes were now fixed upon me, some in mingled respect and astonishment. One fellow armed with a long knife broke the silence and told them to ask me who I was and whence I came. No one, however, seemed to dare to question me. A few minutes afterwards a chief servant of the Khan, armed with sword, dagger and pistol, came out and quietly beckoned me away to a well-furnished guest-house. Here a sumptuous repast was soon prepared, and the two Khans and several others with myself all sat down. The Khan of Lalpura always carried about in his belt a double-barrelled pistol and dagger. After the meal was over he told me very kindly if I was tired I could retire to rest.

"The next morning I spoke to the Khan of Jelalabad about his saying I was a mullah from Bokhara. I said it was better to be killed than to have all those lies told about me. He said that he did not think it prudent to say who I was till he had given me over to the Khan of Lalpura. The next day before all his court I was formally handed over to the Khan of Lalpura, who took me up, seated me beside him, and said, 'We are friends now.' During a pause in the business of the morning court I asked the Khan of Lalpura if I might say a few words to the assembled court and soldiers. He very kindly gave me leave to do so. I then addressed them, and said I was not an emissary of the British Government, or in any way connected with it, that my work was one of love, that many of the mullahs seated there were acquainted with our religion. 'What great crime have I committed that I have been born an Englishman? God has ordained it so.' The day then passed very pleasantly, for I had religious conversation with some of the mullahs. The next day the Khan, with a large company of soldiers, flags flying and drums beating, set out with me for the borders of British territory, which we reached on the third night. During our march we gained accessions at every village until there were 600 men all armed to the teeth. The fourth morning the Khan took leave of me, accompanying me to the river. Here the unfortunate man who had taken the rupee from me on starting was found out, as he had not shared it with his companion, and his life was threatened. They said they would let him off this time on my account. I begged them to keep their word, and in order to ensure his life, I gave another rupee to the principal man of the ferry. From the ferry the Khan sent me on to British territory under an escort of three of his principal men, besides footsoldiers. No sooner had I arrived in the peaceful confines of British territory than, taking off my turban and shoes, I knelt down and thanked God for bringing me back in safety. One of them said, 'God is King; He preserved you.' Another said, 'Your Book' (*i.e.*, Bible) saved you.' I ought to mention that some of the villagers near British territory spoke very kindly to me, saying, 'How do you like our country? Which suits you best?' I said, 'If you will let me stay, yours does.' Others said, 'Come as often as you like.' I said to one of them, 'I was told that if you had known there was a Feringhee in the kafilah you would have cut me to pieces.' He replied, 'Who said that?' I parried the question and said, 'The whole kafilah.' He said, 'We would not have killed you, but kept you a prisoner till we heard from Sher Ali Khan or the British Government.' I was then conducted to Peshawar, and here ends my narrative."

More than twenty years after another attempt to cross the frontier was made by Mr. Jarvis and Mrs. Jarvis, of the Faith Mission, Lahore. Mr. Jarvis has kindly sent the following account of this attempt:—

"It was early in the year, 1895, while doing missionary work in Bombay that the Lord called us to work on the frontier, and the thing was made so clear to us that we had no doubt about our call to those frontier fields.

"We reached Hoti Mardan on July 24th the same year, and pitched our tent under some shady trees in the cantonment, where we visited the people and studied the Pushtu language, all the time making preparations to reach Chitral. Our aim was to reach the Kafirs, an independent non-Muhammedan tribe who had called for missionaries, but none had gone. This was before they were captured by the Ameer of Afghanistan and forced into Muhammedanism. We wrote to the Viceroy for the necessary permission; this he refused. I next saw the Commander-in-Chief as he passed through Hoti Mardan with his staff. He was very kind and sympathetic, but said he could not help us, as it was beyond his power.

"We next wrote to the commandant at Malakand, asking for permission to cross the frontier. This he refused. We prepared to cross without permission, hiring two Ekkas (country carts without springs and drawn by one horse) to take us as far as possible. Six mules had already been sent on two days ahead and were waiting for us.

"We left Hoti Mardan at 9 p.m. one dark night, travelled all night and next morning we were arrested as we were entering the Swat Valley.

"We were met on the road by the Political Officer* with a bodyguard of troops from the Regiment of Guides stationed at Hoti Mardan. Some of these men recognised us, and, we think, told the Political Officer, who at once sent troops to bring us back.

"The Political Officer treated us very kindly, put his own suite of rooms at our disposal, and in the evening sent us back to Hoti Mardan under escort."

*The late Sir H. A. Deane.

An Afghan Heretic

CHAPTER VIII*

WHEN Alexander the Great came into the region of the confluence of the Swat and Cabul rivers, he found a tribe of people there who called themselves, as Arrian records, the name "Aspasioi." If we ask the people in the same region at the present day what great tribe they belong to, they reply, "to the Aspzoi." The Greeks then were pretty accurate in their rendering of this native name, much more so than nations who subsequently came in contact with this tribe. The Mohammedans are indeed in the habit of changing foreign names so that they may in some way fall in with their own traditions; and if such foreign name contains a letter not known in classical Arabic, such letter is almost uniformly replaced by the corresponding Arabic letter; g is changed into j, p into f. Hence a tribe of Afghans adjoining the Aspzoi, the Gadun tribe, is known in documents usually as the Jadun tribe. In Kashmir, for instance, the Hindu deity, Kasyapa, who is said to have drained off the lake which once covered the beautiful valley, was changed by the Mohammedans into one Kashaf, a skilful minister of King Solomon's, who performed this task. This name was so much the more readily chosen as it is connected with Arabic and Persian roots which mean "to open" and "to split." They found in Kashmir a temple called after one Sandhiman,

*For the contents of this chapter the author is much indebted to a paper by the late Isidore Lowenthal.

the minister of one of the Hindu kings of the country. This name was readily changed into Sulimán, the Arabic form of Solomon, and the hill on which the temple is built is now known under the designation of "Solomon's Throne."

In like manner the name "Aspzoi" was readily transformed into Yusufzoi, and so much the more speedily adopted by the literate portion of the tribe, as it changed the heathen "sons of a horse" into noble "sons of Joseph," and thus seemed to free them from what is deemed among Mahommedans the greatest reproach, that of being the "sons of burnt fathers," *i.e.*, of unbelievers, by making them the sons of Joseph one so renowned in the East as a true believer. The illiterate, however, know nothing of this grand name and continue to call themselves "Aspzoi" or "Asupzoi." "Yusufzoi" or "Yusufzai" is the name by which this tribe of Afghans has become known in Europe. The tribe is a large one and inhabits the wild plain north of the Cabul river, and a portion of the adjoining valleys of Swat and Buneir.

In characteristics they differ little from other Afghan dwellers in the plains. Not so thievish or savage as the banditti of the mountains, they still show sufficient affinities with the other tribes to be known as true Afghans—be it in the multitude of their vices or the paucity of their virtues. The Asiatic trait of untruthfulness is common to them all. It is this which becomes the source of unending litigiousness among the men and of unfaithfulness among the women. It makes the missionary also doubly suspicious of any one of them who presents himself as an enquirer. The notion of loyalty (except perhaps in military service) seems to be one wholly foreign to their modes of thought and feeling. High and low among them seem to think it no disgrace, much less a violation of conscience, to break the most solemn oaths and engagements if self-interest appears to demand it.

They usually make a good impression at first on a stranger by their apparent frankness and hospitality. But their hospitality is more the result of a prevailing fashion than of genuine feeling, and their frankness is very frequently a most skilfully devised cover for duplicity.

The Yusufzais have long had the reputation of being one of the most warlike of the Afghan tribes, but all Afghans possess the attribute of physical bravery. The Yusufzais have come more in contact with successive invasions whether Greek, Moghul, Sikh or English than most other tribes, and this has made them better known. They are a teeming tribe, and are to be found in thousands in the service of every native chief from Kashmir to Hydrabad in the Deccan.

Fanaticism and superstition, however, are qualities for which they were known to deserve a bad pre-eminence even among the Afghans. In the earlier days of British rule in Afghan territory a man's reputation for being an orthodox believer and faithful follower of "The Prophet" was forfeited at once by his taking service under the Government. A servant of unbelievers is an unbeliever himself. And many a blood feud arose from the opprobious terms applied by Afghans to a fellow-villager whenever he ventured to revisit his home after having "taken the shilling." Riots even took place when it was attempted to inter in Mohammedan burying grounds those who had died in British service. Men on their death-beds have been known to renounce their allegiance to the British Government and have begged that their names might be erased from the rolls of the service or the regiment to which they happened to belong. At the present time, however, the eagerness among nearly all classes to be employed in some capacity by the Government has become too great and too general for people to manifest their fanaticism, however much they may still indulge in religious hatred. One of the missionary's trials is to be continually pestered with requests for "sifarish" (or recommendation for employment to some Government official) by his out-of-work Afghan friends. Nothing will persuade them that with the ordinary Anglo-Indian official a recommendation from a missionary would rather tell against a man than otherwise.

Their superstition is probably the greatest obstacle which the missionary encounters amongst them. Their religion must be true they maintain as there are such holy men ("Buzurgs") among them that they can work miracles. They tell of a certain man, who has read a particular elegy, the "Qasida Suriani," by Abd Allah ibn Abbās, ten thousand times ; hence he is able to make a man's head fly off his shoulders by waving his finger. The power of superstition is perhaps most signally manifested by the remarkable reverence paid not long ago to the Akhund of Swat (mentioned in a previous chapter) who lived in a narrow valley to the north of the Yusufzai plain. This man, Abdulghafur by name, was residing in a village on the banks of the Kabul river, when the Afghan frontier came into the possession of the Sikhs. He disdained to be under the rule of unbelievers, and emigrated into the nearest country beyond their sway as a fakir or religious mendicant. This step gained him a great reputation with the Yusufzai and other Afghan tribes, and it soon became the custom for people to make pilgrimages to his abode in order to obtain his blessing—a practice which sprang out of an old Hindu custom, and like many other heathen customs, has come down to them from their ancestors.

In the course of time the Akhund gained renown as a marvellous wonder-worker, and that probably much more because the people deceived themselves than because the Akhund endeavoured to deceive them. They have a craving for the marvellous and they deceive themselves much rather than not be deceived at all. It was believed of him that he could change stones into silver and gold; that he could feed thousands every day though he did not possess an acre of land; he gave one man four pence which produced enormous riches; the four original pence were never expended. For whatever people wished they went to him: reconciliation with offended friends, revenge on powerful enemies, a prosperous issue of a doubtful undertaking, even offspring—everything was asked of him. The power he acquired in this way he was reported always to have employed for good objects. He issued decrees against the custom so common among the Afghans of selling their daughters to the highest bidder.

In British Yusufzai, however, and in a portion of Boneir a rival saint made his influence felt, and at one time bid fair to detach numbers of people from their superstitious reverence for the Akhmund of Swat. This man, Synd Amir, a descendant of Mohammed, lived in British territory at the village of Kotah near the Indus. His fame rested upon his great learning, combined with unassuming manners and great sweetness of temper. He was early pronounced a heretic by the mighty Akhund, and as such a verdict from his mouth was equivalent to a sentence of death; an Afridi soon undertook the religious duty of trying to despatch the Mullah of Kotah. He only succeeded in stabbing him severely in the face. When his followers were about to take summary vengeance on the assassin, the Mullah stopped them, spoke kindly to the man, represented to him how wrong it was to endeavour to murder a man who had never injured him, and dismissed him without more ado. This act of forgiveness established his reputation widely among his own people, among whom the virtue of forgiveness is almost totally unknown. He acquired a party which, however, remained secret for the most part because the great Akhund cursed the man and all who followed him.

There is no doubt that his vast reading in Arabic had not remained so totally sterile as is usually the case with Mohammedan scholars. But it is difficult between the falsehoods of his enemies and the ignorance of his friends to make out precisely what peculiar doctrines he held. Some of them are interesting enough. He is said to have denied, for instance, that any mere man can be be an intercessor for another man, whereas the orthodox Sunni belief is that Mohammed's is the only intercession that will prevail at the day of judgment. He held also contrary to the usual belief of Mohammedans that the existing four orthodox sects of Islam are not necessarily the only true ones, but that by a new revelation or by a new interpretation of existing revelations, it is possible for a fifth equally orthodox sect to arise. He opposed the practice of carrying sick and insane persons to the tombs of dead saints in the expectation of miraculous cures. He reprobated the universal practice in their devotions of merely imitating the postures and genuflexions of the Imám or precentor instead of using the prescribed words of prayer.

All his doctrines, however, were not of this enlightened tendency. He is said to have given out that God appeared to him in a vision; he enjoined on his followers a particular position of the forefinger of the right hand when pronouncing the name of God; he allowed them to attach to his name peculiar benedictions.

Other doctrines of his may be inferred from the tenor of a paper which other mullahs required him to sign if he wished to clear himself in the eyes of good Moslems. He tore it up when it was presented to him. The beginning of it was as follows :—

"The learned of every tribe being assembled together, have decided that whosoever refuses to affirm the sole lawfulness of the four legitimate sects, is a prevaricator and a seducer. Whosoever affirms the corporeality of God or the possibility of seeing Him in a vision or a dream or believes in it is an infidel. Whosoever affirms of any individual, except those to whom it has been divinely demonstrated, that he will certainly go to paradise, is an infidel. Whoever speaks against the Khalifs Abubekr and Othmán, or against Imam Hanifa, or against Akhund Darweza (v. chap. iv.) is a prevaricator and seducer; and if he despises those who have fought and laboured for the faith, he is an infidel. Whosoever pronounces the Benedictiou (*i.e.*, the formula 'on whom be peace!') on any but the prophets or the angels is a transgressor. Whosoever says that the dead derive no benefit from the alms and prayers offered for them is a schismatic. Whosoever pronounces any person now living fit to be a prophet is a heretic," etc., etc.

These particulars of the Mullah's history are here mentioned because they explain how it was that he became instrumental in obtaining for the Pushtu Scriptures their first entrance, so to speak, among the Afghans. As the Jewish missionary Lowenthal completed the translation of different portions of the New Testament in Pushtu, he made efforts to get the Afghans to take and read them. These efforts were but rarely successful. The bigotry of the Afghans was in many cases added to a prevailing disinclination to read anything without being paid for it.

In others it was great enough to counteract the inclination where it did exist. Mullahs would follow the missionary as far as forty miles to induce him to take back a Gospel which in a moment of weakness they had accepted and which because of its containing the name of God they would not destroy. One man returned a book because a child of his got sore eyes soon after he had brought the book into the house. Many denied their ability to read rather than expose themselves to the offer of a Gospel. Some young men who had taken the book to the mosque with them and read it there aloud (these people always read aloud) had it taken from them, and were themselves ignominiously turned away. Some men of position by rank and by learning had accepted some books and given evidence of having read them; but they made no parade of their liberal-mindedness, and their example remained comparatively without influence.

It became, therefore, important to do something to interrupt the sad stagnation. The translation of the New Testament had been finished, and these seemed a prospect of nearly the entire edition remaining on Loewenthal's hands. He gives the following graphic account of how the prevailing indifference was broken up:—

"One day our camp was pitched at a short distance from the village of Kotah, the residence of the famous mullah, and I had sent to ask for an interview with him. A polite answer came back that he would be glad to see me in the afternoon. The village is large and full of mosques. I was accompanied by Dr. Bellew, the well-known author of a work on the Afghans. We were led, not into the mullah's house, but into the mosque which he principally frequents, a large one for a village, with its court-yard beautifully shaded by tamarisks, jujube,

Pathans of Yusufzai
(Photographed by Dr. Stein).

and other trees, and freshened by the cool water of a deep well, which occupied one corner of the courtyard. It was a festival day, and the joyous character of the Afghans shone forth conspicuously. They were not at work, and all dressed in their best and cleanest; long white robes principally, with dark blue turbans and scarfs. We had passed crowds of them in the open spaces before the village enjoying themselves in various ways; great big men swinging themselves on swings attached to the boughs of large trees, playing games with astragaloi (bone dice) such as the old Greeks used to play; attending eagerly partridge-fights; eating parched grain and sweetmeats, or lounging about and making a noise simply. There were high and low, old and young, all intent on amusement,—but not a female visible anywhere, not even little girls among the crowds of boisterous boys. We had threaded our way through the merry throng, and had reached the appointed place. A carpet was spread on the spot where the men usually stand during their devotions; two chairs were placed at one end for the visitors, and a bedstead at the other for the Mullah.

"The whole place, as well as the roofs of adjoining houses, was crowded by hundreds of eager spectators and auditors. It was not long before the Mullah made his appearance, walking with a dignified deliberation such as respectable Asiatics are inimitable in. He is a vigorous old man of strong build and erect carriage, with fine bold features, his beard died of a fiery red (in imitation of the traditional colour of Mohammed's); his eyes appeared weak; he kept them shut most of the time. One side of his face is disfigured by a great scar, the mark of the Afridi's dirk and the foundation of his fame. He was well dressed in pure white, and had on his head a white turban of very large dimensions. Leaning on a tall staff and passing the beads of his rosary through the fingers of his right hand, he wended his way slowly through the crowd, men falling down before him and kissing his feet.

"After mutual greetings and customary compliments we took our seats. As soon as we had sat down, the Mullah introduced the interview by a long silent prayer. He held his hands before his face, the palms sloping upwards, and moved his lips. The silence was profound; the people all around held their hands like the Mullah, and when he signified the close of the invocation by stroking his long beard the congregation likewise stroked their beards. After that the conversation began. It was in Pushtu, much garnished with Arabic and Persian quotations. Good manners seemed to require extremely long pauses between the interlocutions. These, on his part, were intended for marks of admiration. Now and then he would give his admiration some audible expression, in which, in each instance, a large part of the congregation joined.

"The conversation was purposely kept as much as possible in a stratum of non-controversial subjects, and after some commonplaces turned on the value of *books* generally; then also on freedom of opinion; on the wrong of certain men presuming to set themselves up as infallible Popes (a hit, probably, at the Akhund!) on the necessity of proving all things, and many similar topics. During the conversation I presented to the Mullah copies of the four gospels in Pushtu. As soon as I produced them he arose from his seat, whereupon all the people likewise, who were sitting on their heels, jumped to their feet. He covered his hands with his scarf, and received the books in his hands thus covered with the greatest reverence. He then kissed the books, placed them on his head, resumed his seat, but, unlike his position previously, drew up his feet also on the bedstead. In this position he again fell into the attitude of silent prayer, and all the people with him.

"After taking the books down from his head, and placing them on a cloth before him, he made various inquiries concerning the New Testament, and concerning the translation of it; and the interview was cut short only by the arrival of the hour for evening prayer; which he, indeed, was too polite to mention, but which I presumed must be near; and the moment we rose the Muezzin struck up his loud call.

"The solemn acceptance by the Mullah of these Scriptures, with his benediction upon them, produced a great change in the temper of the people of the Yusufzai villages. During what remained of the itineration, there was no more necessity of searching for audiences. As soon as my tent was pitched in any place, it was at once surrounded by crowds, who wished to get the now famous books. From morning till evening preaching and distribution had to be kept up, as long as strength and the supply of books lasted. The friends and adherents of the Mullah would have the books because their spiritual guide had taken them: and the far more numerous party of his opponents and enemies wanted the books to obtain corroborative evidence of the heretical tendencies of the Mullah.

"The Mullah himself some months later found the storm he had raised against himself by his liberality too much even for his weather-beaten head. In order to establish his standing for orthodoxy, he began to make preparation for a pilgrimage to Mecca. This somewhat conciliated his detractors; and as soon as the hubbub had subsided, he remained quietly at home.

"He evinced his enlightened liberality lately again, when a native Christian, a Yusufzai also, who is suffering much persecution for conscience' sake, visited him. He received him very kindly, and asked him to partake of his hospitality. When the food was brought in, the native Christian asked him whether he was aware that since his baptism Mohammedans would not eat with him. The Mullah replied he knew it well, and that it was ignorance and inhuman hatred which produced such a feeling towards him, the Christian; that he, the Mullah, considered his leavings "lawful." Those only who have been in the East can fully understand the extent of this liberality. He then made him sit on the same couch with him, and broke bread with him before many people."

Six years after Mr. Loewenthal's visit the late Bishop (then Mr.) French made a tour in Yusufzai. Referring to the same Mullah, he wrote: "The Mullah of Kotah is now a very aged man and has done the English good service by his friendly bearing towards them, and by causing his sons to enlist in their service and other still more important good offices. It was an affecting interview with the old man. In the well-shaded court fronting his mosque his disciples (talibān-i-ilm) were scattered in groups of two and threes bending over the various religious or philosophical authors they were studying. He received me in a darkened room at the corner of the little enclosure, where he sat, all but blind and too infirm to rise, propped on rezzais (thick native blankets), and pillows, surrounded by a large gathering of mullahs and disciples, to whom he was an object of almost devout reverence. I proposed for consideration the best means of attaining to and increasing in the love of God. The whole audience of course in his presence listened with earnest attention. He heard me through and said little but that these were deep truths, which all could not comprehend or receive. He made no opposition, however. There was a most impressively calm and dignified bearing about him. I found in my after-journeyings the most marked differences between those villages and towns where he was the object of reverence and where the Akhund of Swāt was held in honour." The effect of Syud Amir's influence was still visible when the writer visited that part of Yusufzai about thirty years later in 1901. The Khan of the neighbouring village of Zeyda kept copies of the Scriptures in Urdu, Persian, Arabic and Pushtu in his house, and at Kotha Syud Amir's son and successor was quite friendly and willing to converse. In fact, the generally mild bearing of the Khans and Mullahs of Yusufzai towards missionaries causes them to be stigmatised by the more bigoted Muhammadans of the city and its neighbourhood as "Christians." They are still far from that, but Yusufzai, from the missionary point of view, appears to be the most promising section of the Peshawar Frontier.

"Two Soldiers of the Guides"

(From the "Church Missionary Intelligencer")

CHAPTER IX

IN 1859, as one of the missionaries at Peshawar was returning from preaching in the streets of the city, a native policeman came up to him and made some enquiries concerning Christianity, It then appeared from his statement that he had been in search of truth for some time, having read Dr. Pfander's celebrated work, the "Mizan-ul-Haqq" (Balance of Truth), which had been placed in his hands by Dilawar Khan*, the Christian subadar of the Guide Corps. The missionary the following day gave Fazl-i-Haqq a copy of the New Testament and placed him under instruction. After a delay of some months he was baptized with his former name, Fazl-i-Haqq, meaning "the grace of truth."

At that time Fazl-i-Haqq was a policeman. There were, however, difficulties in the way of his remaining in the police as a Christian, at that critical period of his life, and he was urged by the missionaries to take service in some way connected with the mission until his Christian character had become more formed. He, however, declined the offer, saying, "If I remain with you then the people will say I became a Christian for temporal advantages." He soon took his discharge from the police and enlisted into the foot regiment of the Guide Corps, in which his friend Dilawar Khan was a

*For an interesting account of Dilawar Khan v. Col. Younghusband's "Story of the Guides," Macmillan & Co. Also note at end of this chapter.

subadar, and regarded both by officers and men as a brave and good soldier. Through the protection of this brave man Fazl-i-Haqq was enabled to make a bold profession of his faith, and from that moment his father, a mullah at the village of Adina, near to Mardan, where the Guides were stationed, disowned him and refused to see him. In 1864, however, the enmity of the native officers, and particularly of the subadar in command of his company, became so great that his life became almost a burden to him, and he resolved to leave the regiment. It was then that the strong desire took possession of his mind to visit Kafiristan, that curious enclave in the middle of Afghanistan, peopled by the Siah-posh Kafirs ("black-coated infidels"), who were supposed to be partly descended from Alexander's Greek soldiers, and who had remained as isolated idolaters, though surrounded by fanatical Afghan Moslems. There were some Kafir soldiers in the Guide Corps whom Colonel Lumsden, the commandant of the Guides, had brought from their own country and persuaded to take service with him. Fazl-i-Haqq was much thrown with them, for they, like himself, were regarded as outcasts by their Muhammadan comrades. He had taught some of them to read the Gospels in Pushtu, and often spoken to them of Christianity.

They had no settled faith of their own, and proved willing listeners; they also urged him to go to their own country to tell their own people what he had taught them. Two of them had gone on leave to Kafiristan, and from thence they sent him another message telling him to come. The desire to do as they asked fixed itself deeply in his mind, and nothing could turn him back from his purpose. He knew the difficulties of the undertaking, for he was a Pathan himself, whom the Kafirs regarded as deadly foes and were always plotting to kill. During the Umbeyla war of 1863 he had gone alone to Boneir as an emissary for the British Government, who trusted him to bring reliable information in a way that they could not trust Muhammadans. There he had been discovered to be a Christian, and had barely escaped with life.

Another Christian convert, Nurullah, also from Yusufzai, who had himself been a mullah and a Hafiz (*i.e.*, able to repeat the Koran by heart), agreed to accompany him. They were supplied with medicines from the medical mission fund, and also with many little presents for the people.

On the 8th September, 1864, the two Afghans left Peshawar. They were obliged to go as simple travellers, for there is a wide belt of Muhammadanism between Peshawar and Kafiristan inhabited by Mohmands and other fanatic tribes where travelling is dangerous at all times, but where it is ordinarily death to be known as a Christian. They could only travel therefore as other Afghans did, but when once arrived in Kafiristan, they hoped to appear in their proper character. They had arranged in Peshawar with the leader of a caravan to conduct them to Jelalabad, but he had been told that they were Christians, and declined any connection with them whatever. They determined, therefore, on another route, and struck out boldly to the north instead of the west, through Swat and Bajour, on a road not much frequented even by natives, and altogether unknown to Europeans.

They left Peshawar quietly and arrived the same night at a village called Kangra, where, however, they were again discovered by a pupil of Fazl-i-Haqq's father, who was a Mullah. He abused them as Christians, and threatened to expose them. Fortunately he could do no more, for they were still on British ground. On crossing the frontier and entering Swat they walked a few miles with their baggage on their shoulders when they saw two men whom Nurullah knew, one of them having been a pupil in the Peshawar Mission School. They turned into some rice-fields and succeeded in avoiding observation, but had to wade ankle-deep in water to the Swat river, which they forded with difficulty. After a march of more than twelve hours they reached Bar Badwan, where a hospitable potter took them in and gave them food.

On the 12th September they arrived at Kalumanai. The road was considered dangerous, but they obtained two armed men for a guard. The following day they left Swat behind them and entered Bajour, after crossing the Malagi river, which they did in a cradle drawn over the torrent by means of a rope bridge. They halted at Walai, and, being much fatigued, fell asleep under a tree, but were soon woken up by another disciple of Fazl-i-Haqq's father, who wanted to know what he, a Christian, was doing there. They tried to pacify him with friendly words, and gave him a present of a small Birmingham looking-glass; but he demanded ashrafees (gold coins) and pearls as the price of not instantly giving information that they were Christians and having them put to death. He was at last conciliated with nine rupees, and finding that he was ill with dysentry, they gave him medicine, which relieved him, and he then took them to his uncle's house and gave them food. After leaving Bajour and entering Kunar they crossed the Hindooraj, an exceedingly high mountain clothed with forest on its north-west side. The first village in Kunar was Marawurm, where they were only two marches from the Kafirs, a party of whom had attacked the village two nights before and killed a man and woman. They found the people excited and keeping nightly guard in expectation of another attack. The two travellers were told either to watch with them or to leave their village. They sat down with them, and the following conversation with a mullah occurred: " Where do you come from ? " " From Yusufzai." " From what village ? " " From Adina." " Do you know Mullah Pasanai ?" (Fazl-i-Haqq's father). " Yes." " Did you ever see his son Fazl-i-Haqq, whom I knew as a child when I was the mullah's disciple ? " " Yes." How are they all, are they well ? " " Yes, they are all quite well." " Then come in," said the mullah, " and have something to eat, for you have brought me good news." He made the people let them go, after payment of a few pice, and got them some food.

Four Sowars (armed horsemen) who were going on their road were their escort to Kunar. They here crossed the Kunar river on inflated skins. On reaching Bariabad in Ningrahar they saw a few students from Yusufzai whom they knew well, sitting in a mosque as they entered the village. They retired without being observed, and meeting a man outside the village with camels and covered Kajawas, such as are used by veiled women on their journeys, they bargained with him to take them concealed as women to Jelalabad, giving as their reason that they had enemies in the neighbourhood whom they wished to avoid.

Thus they reached Jelalabad in safety. They had travelled on unfrequented roads some 150 miles, in order to avoid the direct road through the Khyber Pass, which would have been only about seventy miles, but was felt to be impracticable for them, infested as it was by the murderous Afreedees. They did not, however, think it safe for them to remain long at Jelalabad, so after one good dinner of meat and melons and grapes they entered at once on their further journey. They now entered a country on the banks of the Mungo river, where every man's house is a fort and every village a castle; and they proceeded onwards by successive marches to Kajgara, the village of another soldier of the Guides who was their friend named Shahbuddeen. They gave him a Peshawar turban and cured his little daughter who lay sick with fever, and he accompanied them to Niliar, the last Muhammadan village on their way. Here dwelt Abdullah, the son of a Kafir chief, who was a great man in that neighbourhood, being the principal channel of communication between the Kafirs and the Muhammadans. He frankly told them that if they entered Kafiristan they would both be killed. They said they had friends there and gave him presents to induce him to accompany them with seven guards to Malel. The road was exceedingly steep, so that they could only climb the hill by clinging to the rocks with hands and naked feet. From Malel Abdullah and Shah-buddeen returned, being afraid to proceed further, and Fazl-i-Haqq and his companion were left alone in the Kafir country.

They had now at least attained the object of their journey, and saw the people face to face whom they had endured danger and hardship in endeavouring to reach. They knew that death was the fate of every Afghan Muhammadan in Kafiristan, and they were in the dress of Afghans.

Nurullah was in great alarm, but Fazl-i-Haqq encouraged him. Being in want of food, they bartered four yards of a turban for bread and cheese, money there being of no use and perfectly unknown. Seeing a woman with sore eyes they gave her medicine; she was benefited by it, and soon the whole village brought out their sick to be healed. Six men out of eleven were cured of fever with quinine, and the people became most friendly.

They had then time to look about them. The mountain tops were bare and bleak, but their sides were covered with forest-trees, especially fir; there were also walnut, mulberry, and amluk trees. The fields were artificial, built up in small terraces with stones. The houses were many of them five stories high, with flat roofs and wooden doors, the people ascending from one story to the next on single sloping beams with rough steps cut in them. Fires were lighted in the centre of the rooms, and they all sat round them, leaving the smoke to escape as it could.

Three days afterwards one of their two Kafir friends who had sent Fazl-i-Haqq the invitation to come to Kafiristan arrived, to their great relief. He had run, he said, the whole way, fearing they would be killed. He had expected some English missionary to be with them, but no English missionary had ventured (though more than one had often wished) to take that road. He showed them the greatest cordiality, begging them to go on to his village and undertaking to defend them with his life.

A fearful initiation into their work now lay before them, exhibiting Kafir ferocity in its worst features. The next march was to Nikera. They here found twenty-eight armed Muhammadans who had been invited by the Kafirs over from Mungoo. It was many years since a number of Kafirs had been slain in their village, and they thought the fact forgiven or forgotten and thought themselves quite safe when they came armed and in such numbers to accept the Kafirs' hospitality. Their hosts feasted them bountifully, and after dispelling all suspicion from their minds, had persuaded them to leave their arms in the huts assigned to them. At this time the two travellers arrived and had a long conversation with the Afghans from Mungoo, two of whom were mullahs and six students from Kunar, when suddenly their Kaffir friend called out to them in Hindustani to come away. "What for?" they asked. "Because they are going to dance." "Then we too will stop and see it." "But there will be a scene (tamasha), and you must come away."

They withdrew quietly and sat down on a rock above. The Kafirs brought a drum and pipes and began to sing and dance, throwing their hands and feet about, the women looking on. Then suddenly, without one moment's warning, each Kafir knife was unsheathed and seen poised high above his head, and with a loud whistle four or five Kafirs rushed on each Muhammadan, stabbing him in every part. The whole was over in a moment, and all had sunk down dead, covered with many wounds. They then beheaded them and threw them all down into the river below. Fazl-i-Haqq and his companion were speechless with horror, when Ghara, their Kafir friend, again told them not to fear, for not one hair of them should be touched. They pointed to the dead bodies below, and gasped out that they too one short quarter of an hour before had been the Kafirs' guests. He told them the reason of such dreadful vengeance. The blood feud was still unremoved, and the Kafirs had never forgotten their own brethren murdered long before. Three days after the Kafirs sent to Mungoo to tell them to send men for the property of the slain, for Kafirs never plundered but only killed the Afghans. Some people went from Malel and brought back their muskets and daggers (which the Kafirs so much valued, but could not take), and also their heads or hands.

From Nikera they proceeded to Ghara's own village, Shaiderlain. Here they met many Kafirs who had formerly taken service in the Guide Corps, and who hailed them as friends, bringing their wives and children. Missionary work was now carried on in earnest for about twenty days. All day long from morning to night they were talking with the people and answering questions, and were joined by them in their services. At night they wrote their journal, giving in Pushtu a full account of all they saw and heard with names of persons, places, and things. This journal was written with lime-juice, and on their return appeared to be only blank pages of white paper, but, when heated over the fire, the letters gradually darkened, and assumed their proper shape. Ghara and his wife were the most interested, but all listened and all applauded as Ghara translated into the Kafir language what was spoken. At times the whole village, men, women, and children, were assembled together. They had great faith in the supposed healing powers of Fazl-i-Haqq and his friend. A girl one day brought her little brother, who was crying from a bad attack of toothache, asking them to pray for him. They did so, and stroked his face. The girl thought he was cured and led him away, and on the child beginning again to cry, she slapped his face, for crying, she said, after he had been healed. Whether it was nature, or the blow, the child was healed, and his recovery being attributed to their prayers, they all brought their implements—a gun, or plough, or bow and arrow—to be blessed.

As the winter approached, the two Afghan missionaries had to decide between spending the winter there or returning home. For many reasons it appeared right for them to return. Ghara and many Kafirs accompanied them for four days' journey on their way to Malel, where they sent them safely out of Kafiristan. They travelled by the old road to Jelalabad, and thence by water on a raft down the Cabul river to Peshawar after two narrow escapes from the Imam of a well-known mosque in Peshawar, whom they saw and with difficulty avoided, and from a student who recognised them, but was persuaded to keep their secret. They arrived in Peshawar on the 10th of November after an absence of rather more than two months, bringing with them a bow and arrow, a knife, a leathern bottle of wine, boots, girdles, and different parts of the Kafir dress.

They also brought a letter addressed by the Kafirs to the missionary at Peshawar, which ran as follows: "We were very much delighted when Fazl-i-Haqq and Nurullah arrived; but we had hoped that you yourself would have come with them. We were made very happy by the stay they made with us; but when snow began to fall we sent them away for fear that they would be troubled with the cold. But if the winter had not been approaching we would not willingly have let them go. But they have promised to return next summer to us and tell us much more about Christ's religion. Be kind to us therefore, and send them again next summer, and as long as we live there shall be no danger of their death in Kafiristan."

As mentioned in Chapter I., the Ameer Abdurrahman anticipated the missionaries and annexed Kafiristan in 1895. In the interval another Afghan convert, Syud Shah, had found his way there, and been hospitably received, but no European had been able to go.

After Fazl-i-Haqq's return from Kafiristan the missionaries requested him to continue in connection with the mission, in order that he might receive a good education and become better fitted for mission work. It was, however, found that he was not suited for a studious life, and in 1868 he enlisted into the cavalry of the Guide

Corps. Although his regiment was stationed at Mardan, thirty miles from Peshawar, he often used to ride over on the Saturday afternoon, in order to be present at the church service on Sunday.

A short time before he rejoined his regiment he was spending the day with the missionary in charge of the native church; it happened to be the day of the week for the evening church service. The rain was pouring in torrents, and as the majority of the congregation resided some distance from the church the missionary thought perhaps it would be better not to have the service that evening, and proposed sending word to the Christians that they had better worship God at their own homes that evening in consequence of the inclemency of the weather. Fazl-i-Haqq, with an earnestness for which he was remarkable, exclaimed, "Sir! why should we not go? If we had to visit our ruler should we not go? Then why not go through the rain, heavy as it is, to worship God in His house? The Muhammadans," he continued, "will go miles on a Friday to assemble in their great musjid (mosque), and surely we Christians can do it." The missionary felt severely rebuked, and resolved in future to allow nothing to interfere with the regularity of the services.

On another occasion, at the risk of his life, Fazl-i-Haqq tore down a placard against Christianity which had been fixed up in the Peshawar bazaar, and came with it under his arm to the missionary, saying, with a smile, "I've got it!"

A few months after he rejoined his regiment symptoms of disease showed themselves, and he became completely prostrated. In May, 1868, he requested that he might be sent to one of the Peshawar missionaries who was on leave of absence in the hills at the time, and after a long journey he arrived at Abbottabad and was conveyed to one of the regimental hospitals. He continued in a weak state for some days. He was frequently visited by the chaplain and several officers who knew him, as well as by the missionary. A short time before his death the missionary said, "Fazl-i-Haqq, you have received much persecution for Christ's sake, now tell me are you sorry you became a Christian?" He earnestly replied in a manner that showed he felt hurt by the question, "How could I be?"

He died on a Sunday morning and was buried in the pretty little Christian cemetery at Abbottabad. His remains were followed to the grave by the only native Christian in the place (a learned Moulvie of Amritsar), the chaplain of the station, and an officer in command of one of the batteries of artillery.

NOTE ON DILAWAR KHAN.

The above account of Fazl-i-Haqq may be fitly supplemented by that of the baptism of Dilawar Khan, his friend and fellow soldier, which occurred exactly fifty years ago—June, 1858. Dilawar Khan has been brought perhaps into greater prominence than any other native Christian, a whole chapter being devoted to him in Colonel Younghusband's "Story of the Guides." But this, of course, deals with him chiefly as a soldier. The circumstances which led to his baptism are narrated in the following letter from a missionary stationed at Peshawar in 1858: "I have been highly privileged in baptizing the first Afghan convert of this mission, and send you a short narrative of the event. Dilawar Khan, the person I have baptized, is a native of a village on the Peshawar border and of pure Afghan blood. Like all his race, he is a tall, manly fellow, not less than six feet high, and at the present time his age may be forty-two. He was for some years a 'Border Robber,' and thought he was doing God service when, at the instance of his mullahs, he plundered Hindu traders. It is not unlikely that in years gone by he laid some of those he regarded as 'Kafirs' (infidels) low in the dust. He was too independent to bow to every teacher, and did not hesitate to reason with the mullahs upon certain points he could not acquiesce in. At that time or soon after he met with Colonel Wheler, who has been well known in India as an earnest preacher. Colonel Wheler gave him a copy of the Mizan-al-Haqq and urged him to study it. From that time Dilawar Khan entertained serious doubts of the mission of Muhammad and the truth of the Koran. He conversed with Colonel (afterwards Sir Herbert) Edwardes, and was much encouraged by him. Subsequently in 1853 the Peshawar Mission was established, and Dr. Pfander and Mr. Clark came here. Dilawar Khan soon made the acquaintance of Dr. Pfander, and began to acknowledge his doubts of Muhammadanism. He received the Bible and studied it, and as he proceeded in his enquiries he sought the mullahs in several places and asked them to answer the Mizan-al-Haqq or refute the arguments which had satisfied him of the truth of the Gospel. No one could do this, and his faith became stronger and stronger. He was now no longer in doubt and began to accompany Mr. Clark to some of the villages near Peshawar and help him in preaching in Pushtu. This he did, I understand, upon several occasions, and as he is well known, a man of talent, and well-informed, his helping a missionary made a stir among the people. Yet he had not received baptism, and the missionaries waited with anxiety the time when he would come forward as a candidate.

But their faith was tried. The mutiny broke out in May, 1857. Dilawar Khan was a jemadar in the Guide Corps. With that distinguished regiment he went to Delhi, and so quickly did they start, that no opportunity was afforded him for an interview with the missionaries, nor was any account received of him from the time he left till the return of his corps in February, 1858. He was one of those who survived that terrible struggle; one fourth at least of his comrades died, but he escaped without a single wound, and not only so, but obtained promotion to the rank of subadar.

We might have feared for this inquirer that amidst such exciting scenes he would be tempted to put away his doubts and forsake his new religion. He had no one to encourage his Christian faith; but he held it fast. The only book he had was a controversial one; and from it he gathered arguments against the Mussalmans. You will wonder that he had not taken his Bible with him, but this is easily accounted for by the extraordinary march the regiment made. They started at six hours notice and marched direct to Delhi at the rate of twenty-seven miles a day in the months of May and June!

In the intervals of battles and watches Dilawar Khan studied the truths of Christianity; and one day in the presence of his fellow soldiers called for a loaf of bread and ate it with a European that all might see he was no longer a Mussalman. When the 'Guides' returned from Delhi they were ordered to Peshawar to receive the public honours they so richly deserved. General Cotton received them at a grand review of the whole garrison, and paid them the highest compliment he could. Dinners were given to the European officers by the General and Colonel Edwardes, and the men of the regiment were also entertained at a public banquet. Then they were sent to their station at Mardan, but before they left Colonel Martin urged on Dilawar Khan the duty of receiving baptism, and thought he ought to ask for a few days' leave for the purpose. His commanding officer was willing to give it when applied to, but he himself thought it better to go on with his regiment and wait a better opportunity, as he himself was then expecting some days more of active service; he promised, however, to come in as soon as possible.

We heard no more of him till May, and almost feared he was putting off the last great step; but he kept his promise, and took the first opportunity of obtaining leave and came to Peshawar. He was baptized on Whit Sunday, and then told us all, sponsors and congregation, how thankful he was. He received the name of Dilawar Masih ("Bold for Christ").

It struck me as an interesting fact that he alone, as I think, of all his regiment, refused to take any plunder at Delhi. He who was formerly a border robber upon principle refused to touch the smallest thing of all the spoils of war. He is the only Christian amongst the hundreds of his corps, and although, as a native officer, he is to a great extent protected from the enmity of his fellow soldiers, yet he must endure many temptations.

Seven years later (1865) the Rev. T. P. Hughes arrived in Peshawar, and has given the following graphic account of his first meeting and intercourse with Dilawar. "He was then a man of about fifty-five years of age, tall and spare, with clear sharp eyes and thin aquiline nose. He gave me a warm welcome to Peshawar, but he added, 'We must not talk about religion, for you have just come out and can know very little of the religious systems of this country." Of course much of my first year was spent in my study endeavouring to acquire a knowledge of the language. As soon as I was able to understand a conversation in Urdu, Dilawar volunteered a bit of advice with reference to missionary action. 'Look here, sir,' said he 'If you think the world is going to be converted by men who sit in their studies with closed doors you are mistaken; you must see the people. Sit under a tree in your garden and receive visitors, and don't shut yourself up in your room.' I did not like this piece of gratuitous advice very much then, coming as it did from a man who seemed to me a semi-savage; but old Dilawar Khan was right. The Afghans are a sociable race, and only those Europeans can influence them who are at all times accessible. 'Fursat nahin' (I have not leisure) and 'Darwaza band' (the door is closed) are as wormwood and gall to the soul of the proud Afghan.

"As soon as I was able to carry on a religious discussion in the vernacular, I found that Dilawar's love of argument and discussion was almost a mania. One evening when I was encamped near his station he came to see me at night, and commenced by asking me to explain the origin and existence of evil, remarking that he thought the universal existence of evil proved that the Creator was evil! I was shocked at such a suggestion coming from one of our native converts, and took considerable trouble to explain matters. Being thoroughly tired, I at last appealed to him for a reply, for he had been listening attentively, and his bright intelligent eyes had been fixed upon me for some time. 'Yes,' he said, 'that is exactly my view.' 'Then why did you trouble me on the subject?' 'Ah!' he replied, 'it is important that you should not be without an answer (la jawab) on any subject, and I thought I would try you,' and then with a thoughtful nod of the head, he added, 'I think you'll do.'"

The rest of Dilawar Khan's career, and his death in the British Government's service in 1869, has been recently so well described in Col. Younghusband's book, "The Story of the Guides" (1908) that it is superfluous to dwell on it here. He was certainly the most remarkable convert which the Peshawar Mission has made during its fifty-five years of existence.

The Frontier Rising of 1897:

The Peshawar Medical Mission

CHAPTER X

NOTE.—Some of the material in this chapter has been taken from the "Pioneer" newspaper, Allahabad.

THE risings on the North-West Frontier are generally sporadic, and the tribes seldom act in unison on account of their mutual jealousies and suspicions, but in 1897 many causes combined to produce an almost simultaneous rising all round the frontier for 400 miles, from Swat to Waziristan. Previous to this emissaries from the Sultan of Turkey, who had been irritated by the remonstrances of England with regard to the Armenian massacres, were reported to have arrived in Cabul, and the Ameer himself had published a volume which strongly urged the duty of jehad or religious war against infidels as incumbent on all Moslems. This book was eagerly circulated by the mullahs on the frontier, and must have inevitably stimulated the fanatical spirit of the wild and ignorant tribesmen. Some of these mullahs had made the pilgrimage to Mecca, and on their return they propagated rumours as to what was occurring in Europe, the defeat of the Greeks by the Turks, &c., of the wildest and most inaccurate character. A significant instance of this was afforded by the letter dated Oct. 25th, 1897, which was found in the house of Mullah Saiyad Akbar, and which contained the information that "Aden, a seaport which was in possession of the British, has been taken from them by the Sultan. The Suez Canal, through which the British forces could easily reach India in twenty days, has also been taken possession of by the Sultan, and has now been granted on lease to Russia. The British forces now require six months to reach India."

Besides these incendiary fabrications, the utterances of British statesmen and of members of Parliament upon questions affecting the status and prospects of Islam and its rulers were reproduced, distorted, and exaggerated. Sections of the hill tribes had permanently settled down in the adjacent British districts, and as they were always in close intercourse with their fellow-tribesmen across the frontier, they were naturally affected more or less by the elements of disquietude and disaffection prevailing among them. Frequency and facilities of inter-communication had thus drawn together all sections, and incitements to Jehad on the common ground of religious fervour, had gained adherents not only from distant parts of the border land, but even on both sides of the British frontier.

In addition to all the above-mentioned causes, the necessary task of delimiting by marks and pillars, in accordance with the terms of the Durand Convention, the spheres of British and Afghan influence, furnished the religious preachers with material for stirring up alarm and jealousy among the tribes, who were thus persuaded to connect the delimitation with ulterior designs upon their independence.

The first outbreak occurred on June 10th, 1897, in the Tochi valley, where Mr. Gee, the Political Officer, had gone to collect a fine from the Madda Khel Waziris. He and his party were treacherously attacked as they sat at a meal prepared for them by the Madda Khels. All the British officers were killed or wounded, and the force had to retreat. There was a running fight over three miles of country, which was only ended by the garrison of the advanced post of Datta Khel turning out to rescue Mr. Gee.

On the 26th of July a sudden attack was made by the Swatis, inflamed by the preaching of a so-called "mad mullah," on the forts of Malakand and Chakdara. Fighting went on all night, and several men and officers were killed and wounded. For a few days the fort was in imminent peril. Reinforcements were hurried forward in spite of the terrific heat, the nature of which may be guessed from the fact that in a force of 700 Sikhs, nineteen died from heat and apoplexy on the road. On July 29th the fourth attack of the tribesmen was repelled. The "mad fakir" was badly wounded in this action, an event which probably did more than anything else to discourage the Pathans. On July 30th the strength of the Malakand garrison was brought up to about 8,000 men, and on August 2nd Chakdara was relieved, the relieving force meeting with strong opposition.

A curious fact afterwards came to light which illustrates the kind of reverence felt by the tribesmen for their mullahs. The "mad fakir's" wound necessitated the amputation of two joints of one of his fingers, and these joints were buried with great ceremony, a standard being placed over them and a shrine erected. The fakir gave out that anyone who had a want or wish had only to pay a visit to the shrine in order to get it fulfilled, and he was believed.

Several stories are told of the individual courage of the Pathans in this rising, and the following is an instance of their extraordinary vitality as recorded by an eye-witness. One of the Bengal Lancers ran a Pathan through with his lance, and being unable to extract the lance, left it, and passed on. The Pathan pulled the lance out, threw it away, and attacked the next man who came up to him, wounding his horse with his sword. He then attacked an officer of the 11th Bengal Lancers, who shot him through the head.

During the pacification of the Swat country the Mohmands between Swat and the Khyber rose and made a raid into British territory on August 7th, near Shabqadr Fort, eighteen miles north of Peshawar. They attacked the Hindu village of Shankargarh and burnt it, killing the only two Hindus who remained there, the rest having fled into the fort, held by a detachment of the Border Police.

On the news of this outbreak reaching Peshawar, General Elles, commanding the Peshawar district, took out a reinforcing column. The Mohmands were driven back by a brilliant cavalry charge and pursued to the foot of the hills, where they took refuge. They were disheartened and made no further demonstration at the time. The mullah of Hadda, who instigated the raid, is reported to have sent a message to the mad Fakir of Swat asking for congratulations, and to have received the answer, "Dog! you have done nothing!" which was in fact the truth.

General Elles and Sir Bindon Blood marching from Shabqadr and the Malakand respectively, burnt several Mohmand villages, though not without some severe fighting. The Mohmand country was traversed in every direction for three weeks; the troops lived free upon the country, which was equivalent to a fine of four thousand rupees a day, seventy-two towers and forty forts were destroyed, and the troops penetrated to the farthest recesses of the mountain fastnesses, hitherto deemed by the clansmen inaccessible to British arms. While these operations were going on in the Mohmand territory, the Afreedees of the Khyber raised the standard of revolt by a sudden and overwhelming attack on Ali Musjid and on Fort Maude, the latter a small fort about three miles from Jamrud and just within the mouth of the Khyber Pass. This fort was held by a detachment of the Khyber Rifles, who, either because they thought they could not prevent it falling into the hands of the enemy, or because they did not care to shoot down their own countrymen, abandoned it and retired to Jamrud, and the Afreedees at once burnt the building to the ground. Advancing further along the pass the raiders came upon Fort Maude. Its little garrison, some forty or fifty of the Khyber Rifles, behaved staunchly, but could not save the situation, for the Khyber was now swarming with Afreedees, whose line extended 1½ miles. At night Fort Maude was seen to be in flames. The post was of no great importance in itself, but there was no telling how far its capture might encourage the Afreedees to press forward. Landi Kotal, the fortified caravanserai above Ali Masjid, was also captured and burnt. Thus, after quietly receiving English subsidies and keeping the road open for seventeen years, the Afreedees had shut up the pass, and the blow to British prestige was great.

In the beginning of the following month (September) the Orakzai rose, and on the 12th captured the small post of Saragheri. The garrison, which consisted of only twenty-one men of the 36th Sikhs, made a gallant defence, holding out from nine o'clock in the morning till 4.30 in the afternoon against odds which from the first were clearly overwhelming. Two determined assaults were brilliantly repulsed, but at the third rush the enemy succeeded in breaking down the door, and when the plucky Sikhs manning the walls rushed down from their posts to defend the doorway, the swarming tribesmen scaled the walls and all was over. But not a Sikh even then thought of surrendering while life remained, and eventually the whole of the gallant defenders fell victims to their heroism.

One stout-hearted soldier in the guard-room killed twenty of the enemy without hurt to himself, and lost his life in refusing to budge when the Afreedees, unable to get at him, finally set the room on fire. The signaller, as brave as the rest, coolly kept up communication with Fort Lockhart up to the very last moment. The details of the fight will never be known, for not a soldier came out of Saragheri alive.

A fund was subsequently opened by the "Pioneer" newspaper, Allahabad, with the object of benefiting the widows and families of the twenty-one fallen Sikhs and of erecting some suitable monument in the Punjab to perpetuate the memory of the defence of Saragheri.

In the meantime the Afreedees had sent a deputation to the Ameer of Cabul asking for help. He refused to receive the deputation, and sent them a written reply, part of which ran as follows: "I do not know on what account a breach has now taken place between you and the English. Now after you have fought with them and displeased them you inform me. I have entered into an alliance with the British Government in regard to matters of state, and up to the present time no breach of agreement has occurred from the side of the British, notwithstanding that they are Christians. We are Moslems and followers of the religion of the Prophet, and also of the four Khalifas of the Prophet: how can we then commit a breach of agreement? . . . .

"I will never, without cause or occasion, swerve from an agreement, because the English up to the present time have in no way departed from the line of boundary laid down in the map they have agreed upon with me. Then why should

I do so? To do so will be far from justice. I cannot at the instance of a few self-interested persons bring ignominy on myself and my people. What you have done with your own hands you must now carry on your necks. I have nothing to do with you. You are the best judge of your affairs. Now you have got into trouble you want me to help you. You have allowed the time what matters might have been ameliorated to slip by; now I cannot say or do anything."

The Afreedees and Orakzai now prepared to resist the advance of the Expeditionary Force into Tirah under Sir William Lockhart. The force advancing from the south took the Sanpagha and Arhanga passes with some loss in men killed and wounded. At the famous storming of Dargai, when a precipitous bluff was taken in the face of a galling fire by the Gordon Highlanders and 3rd Sikhs, followed by the Dorsets and Derbyshires, 163 were killed and wounded. This was the occasion on which Piper Findlater continued to play though shot through both legs.

After enduring great hardships and losses owing to bad weather and the effective marksmanship of the Afreedees, the expedition recovered the Khyber Pass. The Afreedees grew weary of the contest, and gave in their submission to Sir W. Lockhart. With the grim humour of Pathans, numbers of them flocked to the Peshawar station when he left to give him a good send-off! The only real grievance which the Afreedees had, seems to have been that the Government had raised the tax on the importation of salt, which commodity does not exist in their country. Another complaint they made was that their women who had run away to Peshawar were not given back, but this was a matter which the Government could hardly be expected to go into.

The lessons of the Tirah war are well summed up by a writer in the "Edinburgh Review," January, 1898. "It is to timidity of action that many attribute the recent risings, and certainly nothing could have been better calculated to foster the conceit of the ever conceited Pathan than the condition in which the Kohat Pass between two important military stations has been allowed to remain for so many years. We did not even remove the stones and boulders which covered the track, and the tribesmen openly jeered about it. The system in the Khyber could hardly fail to have the same effect. 'That immortal demon, the Khyberee,' as Alexander Burnes quaintly calls him, was paid a large yearly sum for keeping open the pass, but we had no control over the tribe, our officers being forbidden to go off the road. There is, therefore, some ground for thinking that the loss and expense which we have lately incurred were due rather to a want of boldness in our treatment of the tribes than to the forward policy."

When peace was concluded the Afreedees do not seem to have cherished ill-feeling, as numbers of them volunteered for the Boer war, but the Government did not see its way to accept the proposal.

The Peshawar Medical Mission.

This Mission is closely connected with the Frontier War, by the fact that several of its earliest patients were wounded Afghans from Tirah. The great value of medical missions among the Pathans had already been shown by the fact that when the Waziris raided Tank near Bannu they spared the Medical Mission, and Dr. John Williams, the native doctor there, was thanked by the police for the good influence he exercised over the wild tribesmen.

Former Medical Mission Hospital, Peshawar.

The Frontier Rising of 1897

Although the Peshawar Mission was founded in 1853, the women's hospital was not founded till 1883, nor the men's till 1896. In the latter year Drs. Lankester and Browne were sent to Peshawar by the Church Missionary Society. For the comparatively small sum of 2,000 rupees they obtained two large native caravanserais in the heart of the city, within a hundred yards of the place where all the great caravans come in from Afghanistan. One of the first patients was a man from Tirah whose shoulder had been shattered by one of the "Dum-dum" (explosive) bullets. Altogether the number of patients during the first year reached twenty-two thousand.

During the course of 1898 Dr. Lankester was allowed by Sir William Lockhart to open a dispensary at Lundi Kotal, in the Khyber Pass itself. The doctor was allowed to treat the women in the Afreedee villages, and was everywhere received with friendliness and hospitality. During another itineration (in the Khagan valley) he found the women and children flying at the sight of him. This was because they thought he had come to manufacture what they called "Mumiai." According to their belief English doctors enticed young children into their tents, hung them head downwards on a beam above a slow fire, and then collecting an oily matter which dropped from their brains, sold it as a specific for all possible diseases. A few days, however, of medical work dispelled their fears, and Dr. Lankester was everywhere welcomed as a friend.

After the opening of the hospital, each successive year only accumulated proofs that medical work was the shortest way to the Pathan heart. As a medical missionary at another frontier station writes: "Their untutored hearts become touched and they begin to think as to the wherefore of kindness and attention so strange to them. Many come to the conclusion that it must be to win for ourselves a high place in heaven, and therefore it is we who are debtors to them for being the medium by which we attain our object. Hearts that have never been taught the beauty and joy of self-sacrifice are puzzled at a stranger being ready to dress the foulest sores and to wash the dirtiest limbs. Once one of them remarked of one of the workers, 'Ah, if he were only a Muhammedan, he would be an angel!'"

A correspondent of the Pioneer newspaper Allahabad, visiting both the men's and women's hospitals at Peshawar in 1903 wrote the following account in that newspaper: "There are two institutions in the native city which claim the admiration and deserve the support and sympathy of every human being with a heart. One is the hospital for native women under the charge of Miss Mitcheson, the other a Medical Mission under Dr. Lankester. Nothing surprised me more than the cheerfulness, patience, and hopefulness shown by those who are carrying on this grand work of humanity, in the very teeth of hatred, bigotry and fanaticism."

"I went all over Dr. Lankester's wards. There was an old man of sixty with a frightful bullet-wound in his leg. His village is four days' journey away. He was coming into Peshawar when he was shot. Who shot him? Oh, he didn't know; it was all in the day's work. After being shot, he walked on two days' journey to the hospital.

"When Baron Hugel visited Peshawar seventy years ago he saw two men rolling about in the mud groaning in front of Avitabile's house. Their hands had been cut off and the stumps dipped into boiling tar. When I stood in front of Avitabile's house the other day I was thinking of this by force of contrast. There were two English ladies

A Pathan from Ningrahar in the Medical Mission Hospital.

with me who had turned his house into a hospital, and who spent their lives doing good."

A still more weighty testimony was borne to the work by Professor George Adam Smith, who visited Peshawar towards the close of 1903, and wrote: "In the mind of one who for the first time visits that wonderful city and district, missions have to contend with some powerful interests. There is the fascination of seeing about you what is more a part of Central Asia than of India; there are the caravans and bazaars, the strange wild mixture of peoples, the military history of the place and the Khyber Pass. That with such rivals Dr. Lankester's work should more than hold its own in securing the interest of a visitor is perhaps the best testimony I can give to its reality. I was prepared for much by what I had heard of Dr. Lankester's name throughout the Punjab, but I saw with my own eyes much more than I expected. I visited the hospital, saw the out and in patients, examined the registers, and saw besides on our visit to the Khyber with Dr. Lankester the number of wild men who welcomed him for what he had done for themselves or their friends. All this represents an incalculable amount of relief of suffering that must otherwise have remained unrelieved, and were there nothing more I think the Church Missionary Society might feel confident of the value of their mission in these parts."

Professor George Adam Smith, it will be seen, touches upon one of the most important aspects of the Peshawar Medical Mission—its vast influence across the frontier where no missionary is allowed to go. This is borne out by statistics. In March, 1907, out of sixty in-patients, thirty-eight, or nearly two-thirds, had come from trans-frontier districts, and with them were no fewer than thirty-two relatives who were permitted to stay to help with the nursing. Both comic and tragic aspects of the work are not wanting. The comic arises from the ingrained suspiciousness of the Pathan, as in the following instance reported by Mrs. Lankester. "The other day a woman from Central Afghanistan steadily refused to have a bath and clean clothes, and on pressing her for a reason for her objection it was found that she had an idea that a change of clothes meant a change of religion, and that cleanliness involved Christianity! The father of another patient then came to the rescue and assured her that though his daughter had gone through the ordeal of a bath she was still a true Muhammedan."

The tragic aspect arises from the unrelenting persecution to which converts to Christianity are exposed. Not long ago a Pathan woman at Quetta after receiving Christian instruction in the Mission Hospital there, told her husband that she wanted to become a Christian. His reply was to take her across the frontier, where he murdered her.

In 1904, finding the old hospital in the city too cramped and unhealthy, Dr. Lankester, having secured a piece of ground outside the city, began building a new and more commodious hospital. This was opened in February, 1906, the Commissioner of the North-West Frontier Province presiding at the opening meeting. There is little doubt that when the long-closed door into Afghanistan is opened and missionaries are allowed to itinerate there as they do in English territory, many villages will be found to contain those whose first contact with Christianity and civilisation was at the Peshawar Medical Mission.

We may conclude this chapter by quoting from the farewell address presented by the non-Christian inhabitants of Bannu to the medical missionary there on his leaving for furlough after fifteen years of continuous work among them :—

"As a medical man we cannot too highly praise your selfless devotion to our welfare. Without regard to any inconvenience to yourself you have been ready to attend to any call whether from rich or poor at all hours of the day and night. Above all we appreciate and cannot too highly admire your efforts in bridging over the gulf that divides the Europeans and the Indians. It is the men of your stamp that are mostly needed. We bid you adieu and pray for you a happy voyage home. We shall be fondly looking for the day when we shall welcome you back in our midst."

Converts and Enquirers:

An Afghan Martyr

The Rev. W. Thwaites, C.M.S., Mr. A. Brookes, and group of Native Christians, 1895.

CHAPTER XI

IN 1905 a press correspondent, who accompanied the Prince and Princess of Wales to Peshawar, visited the Mission Church in the city and met the native pastor, whom he described, in his account of the tour, as "a gray-bearded Afghan." It was a curious mistake, for the worthy pastor, I. S., is the exact antithesis to an Afghan. He is a Panjabee, and his freedom from Afghan irascibility and quarrelsomeness has enabled him to fill the office of pastor for more than thirty years with acceptability. Born near Amritsar, when a young man he took service with Daud Singh, the first Sikh convert in 1859. Very soon afterwards Daud Singh was transferred to Khairabad on the banks of the Indus opposite Fort Attock, where there was a movement towards Christianity going on among some of the Mazhabi Sikhs of the 24th Regiment.

For some time I. S. continued to be a bigoted Moslem, and would not even drink water out of the vessels of his Christian master. He often heard the Muhammedan religion attacked, and this only increased his bigotry. He felt, however, attracted by some of the doctrines of Christianity, especially that of the Fatherhood of God, which orthodox Moslems consider blasphemous. After considerable mental struggles he opened his mind to Daud Singh and underwent a course of religious instruction. After working for twelve years as an agent of the Peshawar Mission, he was ordained deacon by Bishop

Milman in 1873. Since then he has been Pastor of the native congregation, and has won golden opinions on all sides, being conciliatory and patient in discussions with Muhammadans and free from the quarrelsomeness which too often betrays native Christians into glaring inconsistencies.

In common with all converts from Islam in a Muhammadan city he has had much to bear in the shape of insults and abuse. In one of his reports he wrote: "When the city is filled with strangers from Cabul then it is that our troubles increase. Their desire to persecute us makes them gnash with their teeth, and if we were not most patient in our bearing towards them they would certainly strike us."

One day a Pathan said, "It is in my heart to kill you. I should, of course, be hung for it, but then I should be a martyr" (Shahid). I replied, "A martyr is one who patiently and without resistance suffers for the truth. You wish to use force. Where is the martyrdom in such an action?"

In 1879 I. S. went to Cabul under the protection of the British force to minister to the little flock of Armenians there. He found a very few families who carried on their worship in a very small church, 36 feet by 15 feet. They had communion vessels of gold which they had bricked into the wall to prevent them being stolen. It is indeed remarkable that this feeble witness for Christianity should have been suffered to remain unextinguished in the very heart of Moslem fanaticism. The Armenians also told I. S. that several Afghans have been secretly Christians at heart, and that some of these secret disciples have been buried in the Armenian cemetery. After the Armenian massacres in Turkey the Ameer, probably fearing a similar outburst in Cabul, ordered the

Bihishti (Water-carrier).

Armenians to leave it. Since then they have resided at Peshawar and worshipped with the native Christian congregation.

We come now to the real Afghan converts. The first of these is A. He was, at the time of the writer's residence in Peshawar, the only convert who had come from the mission school. As a youth he was conspicuous for his bigotry. Gradually, however, Christian teaching and influence told upon him, and he was baptised in July, 1884. Just before his baptism he was missed, and the missionary who was about to minister the rite feared he had run away or been carried off, as sometimes happens on such occasions. Going, however into the church compound he found him eagerly disputing with some of his former co-religionists. He was a Government servant in connection with the land revenue, receiving more than he did on becoming a convert so that his conversion was quite free from mercenary motives. For some time afterwards he continued to carry on his duties in a village where he was stationed, but found it impossible, as he was boycotted, the "bihishtis" (water-carriers) even refusing to bring him water. What was even more galling to his proud Pathan nature, his betrothed was taken from him and given to his brother. After this he was sent to study in the Divinity College, Lahore, where he made fair progress in Hebrew and Greek. He then returned to Peshawar, and worked for several years as a catechist. The writer can bear first-hand testimony to his patience, as he has seen him spat upon and roundly abused as a renegade by Muhammadans who lost their temper in argument. When the late Ameer's son, Nusrullah Khan, passed through Peshawar on his way to England, A. went to the bungalow where he was staying with the intention of presenting him with a

Persian Testament, but he could not obtain access to him. Not long ago A. was ordained, being the first Afghan admitted to the ministry. Another Afghan convert belonging to the Peshawar district is K. He was educated at Batala, where the late Miss Tucker (A.L.O.E.) took a great interest in him. On one of his vacations he wrote her a remarkable letter from Peshawar which ran as follows:—

"Janab (honoured) Miss Sahiba, Salaam! The next day after reaching Peshawar I went into the middle of the bazaar, and what did I see? Why, my cousin standing there. When he saw me he ran and embraced me, and shouted and cried so much that I stood in the bazaar astounded. As he was crying he said to me, 'You have dishonoured the whole family; but, still, it is all right. Come to our house, and we will say that you never were a Christian but that your enemies slandered you by saying so.' When I heard this, I cried a great deal, so much so that many Muhammedans came round. Then taking out my Testament I turned to Romans viii. 35 and read, 'Who shall separate us from the love of Christ? Shall tribulation or distress or famine, or nakedness or peril or sword?' Then all the Muhammedans spat in my face and said, 'This is an infidel.' After this other Muhammedans came up, but, turning their faces away, they passed by. You see I am in a place of great temptation; so there is need of great prayer on my behalf."

The case of a third Afghan convert illustrates still more strikingly the difficulty that a proselyte has in remaining stedfast against the strong drift of Moslem bigotry and Pathan public opinion combined. He was of a higher class than the last two mentioned, and owned some land in a village near Peshawar. After four years' study in the

Divinity School at Lahore, he went on a visit to his brother in his native village, where every attempt was made to induce him to return to the faith of his fathers. A few days afterwards the missionary at Peshawar received a letter from him to this effect: "You will soon hear the news; circumstances have been too great for me. On Friday next I shall declare myself a Muhammadan in the mosque, but although I shall openly profess myself a Muhammadan, at heart I am a Christian, and I can never be anything else." Saddened at heart the missionary went to see him, only to hear that the appeal of his friends had been too much for him, and that in a moment of weakness he had yielded. The missionary returned to Peshawar, and two days afterwards to his astonishment he saw the man riding into his garden and said, "Well, what has happened?" He answered, "I am the prodigal returned. When I went back to my village the other evening my brother said, 'You are suffering from some great emotion; whom have you seen? Have you seen the missionary?' I said, 'Yes, I have, and if I must tell you the truth, although I shall declare myself a Muhammedan to-morrow in the mosque, at heart I am a Christian.' My brother said, 'For God's sake, then, clear out of the village; whatever you do, don't deceive those Muhammedan mullahs, for if you do, we shall be slain to a man!' So next morning I left my native village, and here I am, as I said, the prodigal returned."

In 1892 the writer was appointed as a missionary to Peshawar. During his first three and a half years of residence no adult baptism occurred, though he came across some interesting inquirers. Among these was a Muhammedan rissaldar (non-commissioned cavalry officer) who walked with him across the crowded camel-market to the native service in the Mission Church, a bold thing to do in Peshawar. Very different to this man was a mullah who came and sat one Sunday in the writer's bungalow for five hours. On being offered a Pushtu Testament, he asked for pen and ink and copied John xii. 32-36 on a piece of paper, saying he was afraid of accepting a book. Some time afterwards the writer sought him out at his village, and asked him to be his teacher in Pushtu. The next day he appeared with a very lugubrious face at the bungalow, saying, "*Ze yai wahalam*" "They have beaten me." However, he acted as munshi for some time, and would occasionally on leaving stand behind a a tree in the garden if he saw anyone he knew approaching. Altogether he was like Mr. Fearing in "Pilgrim's Progress," and one had to say of him as his guide did of the latter "I lost my man." These cases, where a man, feeling the strong attraction of the Gospel, is again carried away by a stronger undertow of fear of persecution, may be truly called "soul tragedies."

Of another enquirer some time before this, Mr. Jukes, the missionary then stationed at Peshawar, wrote: "There is one man, a Maulvie, spoken of as a bibliomaniac in our last report, who frequently comes for books, and when once he gets into our room of vernacular books it is difficult to get him out of it again, for he has got such an insatiable appetite and has not the money to buy the books. We cannot grudge them, however, for he reads them wherever he goes, and creates a desire for them in others of good birth and education, and reaches a number of people we cannot get at. He has been frequently requested to desist from reading them aloud, but this he has refused to do, as he says there is so much good in our books, and at last he gets them to admire them also, which results in their asking me for more."

In 1896 a real spirit of inquiry seemed to spring up, and

two patwaris (assistants in the Land Revenue Department) having undergone instruction for some time, were baptized. The morning after their baptism the writer going through the city, saw them being chased and hooted by a crowd of the baser sort at their heels. The next month a woman was baptised. She was solemnly cautioned by the native pastor that she would probably have to undergo severe persecution, but the only reply she made was "Ji! ji!" "Yes, yes." After her baptism she returned to her husband, who, however, instead of taking her to his own house put her in charge of a leading Muhammedan in the city, and for more than a month everything possible was done to make her return to Muhammedanism, but without success. It was only when she heard that they were going to sell her over the border that the Zenana lady whose pupil she had been thought it right to get her away to another city where she could live at peace.

We come now to a man who really seems to have been a martyr—possibly the first Afghan Christian martyr—though there may have been others, especially women poisoned in zenanas, etc. This man,* Abdul Karim by name, was first attracted by the preaching of Bishop French in the bazaars of Quetta about 1886. The people insulted and pelted the Bishop, but Abdul Karim took a Persian New Testament from him, partly out of pity. Being a quick reader, both of Persian and Urdu, he became greatly interested. When a clerical missionary was stationed at Quetta at the end of 1887, he soon found him out and went almost daily to read and discuss. After nearly two years he surprised the missionary by an emphatic confession that Christ was right and Muhammad

* *Vide* Letter by the Rev. H. G. Grey, Punjab Mission News, Apri, 1908.

wrong. He asked if he could be baptized secretly; but at once saw that baptism meant confession. He said he must wait until his father, the chief Qazi (judge) of the district, should die. His father did die within six months but Abdul Karim still hung back. Nevertheless, he boldly accompanied the missionaries to villages, and was openly anxious that they should never leave a village without preaching. At last, on Sunday, October 9th, he was baptized. *He immediately had to suffer severe persecution in his own village, and subsequently still greater trials befel him. His wife, who had remained a Muhammedan, was approached by her relations with persuasions to poison her husband or to stab him in his sleep. She however, steadfastly refused, and finally threw in her lot with him and was baptized in June, 1894, and then re-married to him by Christian rite—the Muhammedan marriage having been, according to Muhammedan law, annulled by his baptism.

This only increased the rage of the people. Great efforts were made to induce him to renounce Christianity, and when Sardars, Maliks, and Mullahs found that he, was not to be persuaded by argument or money, it became evident that the only thing they could do was to murder him. Knowing his life to be in danger the Deputy Commissioner gave him a licence to carry a revolver.

At length in October came the attack and defence, only the attack was not made on Abdul-Karim himself but on his wife, and he waking up to see his wife in the grip of her assailant, seized his revolver and shot the man, and then reported the incident to the Deputy Commissioner. The District Superintendent of Police gave his Moslem subordinates a free hand, and they immedi-

*Vide Church Missionary Society's Report, 1895.

ately fabricated a story of their own, and suborned witnesses to show that neither Abdul-Karim nor his wife had been attacked, and that his act was one of cold-blooded deliberate murder. As lawyers are not allowed in Baluchistan the medical missionary at Quetta, Dr. S. W. Sutton, had to turn lawyer to conduct the defence. It was a very arduous task, as the police were determined to bring the man to the gallows.

In the end the Sessions Judge declared that the whole story of the prosecution was a fabrication, and remarked on the terrible amount of perjury which must have been committed. He affirmed that Abdul-Karim was perfectly justified in shooting his assailant, but that he ought not to have fired all the six chambers of his revolver; that he was therefore guilty of "culpable homicide not amounting to murder." He considered that the requirements of the law would be met by a purely nominal sentence of a month's imprisonment. In 1898 Abdul-Karim came to Peshawar, and the writer, having been challenged by the chief mullah of a village near Peshawar to produce a genuine Afghan who had become a Christian, asked Abdul-Karim to accompany him to the village. He did so, and some religious discussion took place between him and the mullah. As they came away Abdul-Karim said that he had overhead a man say, "banduq rawra" (bring a gun!), but this may have been fancy on on his part.

Another missionary writes of him at a subsequent date: "I have known him carry on single-handed a controversial talk with a dozen Muhammadan priests without losing his temper."

At last, after wandering about a good deal, he crossed the frontier into Afghanistan. Whether this was a project which had been simmering in his mind for some time or was a sudden impulse it is impossible to say. A lady missionary, writing from Bannu, thus describes the last scene of his life: "While here he was always more or less restless and wanting to go to Quetta. At length he left us and went there; then he crossed the border, was taken prisoner, and on refusing to repeat the Kalima ("there is no God but God and Muhammad is the Apostle of God") and saying he was a Christian, he was taken to Candahar where the Ameer then was. He questioned him, and on his again refusing to repeat the "Kalima," and saying he had come to preach the Gospel, he was ordered to be flogged, put in chains and to be taken to Cabul, where he was to wait the return of the Ameer, and unless he changed his mind would get due punishment.

"We heard that heavily chained, hand and foot, he set out with an escort to Cabul; that at the villages he was spat upon, and the hairs of his beard pulled out, and at length the poor weary sufferer, at a village before reaching Cabul, was murdered. We have heard that the Ameer, on hearing of the murder, ordered the people of the village to be punished."

In the light of this event, which seems to have occurred towards the close of 1907, some words in an article by Dr. Lankester, contributed to the Propagation Society's quarterly, "The East and the West," seem to be almost prophetic. "To any Oriental Christian who was discovered beyond the frontier the alternatives would speedily be presented of denial of Christ or death. It may be that some of the small group of Pathan or Afghan converts will be constrained by God Himself to go forward and give their lives in witness for their faith."

The foregoing cases to which many others might be added are enough to justify the prophetic words of the

Converts and Enquirers

Rev. R. Clark, the founder of the Peshawar Mission: "We see from history how often Afghans have planted and upheld for centuries the flag of Islam, both in many provinces in India and in many countries beyond it. When they once are Christians they will probably become the most zealous and energetic missionaries of Christianity in Asia."

Persian Influences on the Afghans:

Sufism

CHAPTER XII

IT is a singular fact that Persia, a country peopled by Shiah Muhammadans, situated between Turkey and Afghanistan, which are peopled by Sunnis, their sworn antagonists, has exercised a profound influence upon each. In Persia the conception of God as an austere despot whose chief attribute is merciless power, which is the conception of orthodox Islam, never took deep root. On the other hand, Muhammadan mysticism, which sprang partly from the influence of Christian monks and anchorites in Arabia, and partly from the Neo-Platonism of Alexandria, found in Persia the home of Manes and the early Gnostics, a congenial soil. Just as the Gnostics filled up the gulf between man and God with a chain of eminations or inferior deities such as "Wisdom," "The Abyss," etc., so the Persian Sufis, who also called themselves "Arifeen" (Gnostics or Knowers), were constantly tending to deify human beings like Ali, the fourth Khalifa, to stand as mediators between themselves and the awful remoteness of Allah. This tendency was fostered by the early Sufi teachers, some of whom, like Bayazeed, seem to have come very near to making a claim of divinity. Bayazeed is reported to have said, "Within my cloak there is nothing but God," and Mansur al Hellaj, of Bagdad, was put to death for declaring in a moment of ecstasy "Ana'l Haqq"—"I am the truth."

Of all the Persian Sufis the greatest and the one who has exercised probably the most influence both in Turkey and Afghanistan is Jalaluddin Rumi, of Konia. He was the founder of the Meslevi order, the celebrated dancing dervishes, whose gyrations are intended to symbolize the wheelings of the planets round their central sun, and the attraction of the creature to the Creator. To this day the coronation of the Sultan of Turkey is not considered completed till he is girded with a sword by the head dervish of the Meslevi order in the mosque of Aiyub.

The higher and better side of the Muhammadan mind cannot be understood without some acquaintance with this remarkable writer, of whom pious Muhammadans say " He is not indeed a prophet, but he has a book " (" Paigumbar nest wali dārad kitab "), and of his book itself, the " Masnavi," they say, " It is the Koran in the Persian language."

Jalaladdin Rumi was born at Balkh in Central Asia early in the thirteenth century, and died in 1272 A.D., when Dante was a child of seven. The collocation is suggestive. Dante had probably never heard of the Persian Sufis, but his pilgrimage through Hell, Purgatory and Paradise bears a certain resemblance to the Sufistic stages or degrees of initiation, passed on the journey to the final goal of " wasl " or union with God.

Jalaladdin was brought up at Konia (the ancient Iconium), and it is a curious fact that the Masnavi, his chief work, betrays an acquaintance with St. Paul which is very rare among Muhammadan writers who generally ignore him. Very much in the style of some latter-day critics, he accuses St. Paul of overlaying the simplicity of primitive Christianity with complicated dogmas. Jelaladdin's writings also contain terms borrowed from the Neo-platonic philosophy such as " Aql-i-Kull " for the Logos, and " Nafs-i-Kull " for the Pneuma.

The great mystic endeavoured, as so many have done

since, to separate the husk of dogma from the kernel. He says in a couplet much quoted by free-thinking Muhammadans.

> "I extracted the marrow of the Koran
> And flung the bone to the dogs."

He is perfectly aware that religious belief is based upon an accumulation of probabilities, but in the initiated Sufi's stage of "Hal" or ecstasy he can rise into the sunlight of clear assurance. The cast-iron dogmas of Muhammedanism are molten into universal religious truths in the alembic of his poetry. In his eyes the true Ka'ba is not the tetragonal shrine which the Muhammadan pilgrims perambulate at Mecca, but the human heart. "You may circle the Ka'ba a thousand times," he says, "God cares not for it if you hurt one heart." So with regard to the incessant ablutions enjoined by Islam. "Your hand can wash your body, but what hand can wash your heart?" In this he rises far above the average morality of Muhammadans who dispute whether sins of thought are sins at all.

So again in contrast to the common Muhammadan idea of God as an almighty despot looking with half-amused contempt at the antics of humanity, he says:—

> "Union exists beyond all thought and speech
> Between great Allah and the soul of each,"

and in the following striking apologue he defends the anthropomorphism which orthodox mullahs denounce as rank blasphemy;—

> "Moses, to his horror, heard one summer day
> A benighted shepherd blaphemously pray.
> Lord!' he said, 'I would I knew Thee where Thou art!
> That for Thee I might enact a servant's part;
> Comb Thy hair, and dust Thy shoes, and sweep Thy room
> Bring Thee every morning milk and honeycomb.'

Moses cried : 'O blockhead, curb thy blatant speech,
Whom art thou addressing? Lord of all and each
Allah the Almighty! Think'st thou He doth need
Thine officious folly? Wilt all bounds exceed?
Miscreant have a care! or thunderbolts will break
On thy head, and others perish for thy sake.
Without eyes He seeth, without ears He hears,
Hath no son nor partner through unending years;
Space cannot confine Him, time He is above,
All the limits that He knows are light and love.' "

Put to shame, the shepherd, his poor garment rent,
Went away in sorrow, terrified and shent.

Then God spake to Moses: "Why hast thou from Me
Driven away my servant, who goes heavily?
Not for severance it was, but union
I commissioned thee to preach, O hasty one!
Hatefullest of all things is to Me divorce,
And the worst of all ways is the way of force.
I made not creation Self to aggrandize,
But that creatures might with Me communion prize.
What matter if the tongue trip? 'Tis the heart I see,
If it really opens like a flower to Me.
Blood-stains of a martyr do not washing need,
Some mistakes are better than a cautious creed.
Once *within* the Ka'ba*, wheresoe'er men turn,
Is it much to Him who spirits doth discern?
Love's religion comprehends each creed and sect,
Love flies straight to God and outsoars intellect.
If the gem be genuine, matters the device?
Love in depths of sorrow finds the pearl of price."

Browning, with a poet's intuition, represented the Arab physician Karshish and the Persian sage Ferishtah as alternately attracted and repelled by the doctrine of the Incarnation. In the same way the mystic of Konia felt an irresistible yearning like Plato that Divine wisdom would assume a bodily shape. "Oh that I might

*All Muhammadans pray towards the Ka'ba.

behold," he says, "in flesh the splendours of the Friend!" ("Ta ba-binam dar bashar anwar-i-Yar!") At the same time he rejects the doctrine of the Trinity, the origin of which he ascribes to a kind of theological squint, or seeing God double. Christ to him, however, is something more than the mere human prophet to which the Koran reduces him. "Who could hinder God?" says the Koran, "if He chose to destroy Mary and her son together?" Jalaladdin seems to incline to the Arian hypothesis. "Jesus came in flesh," he says, "but was of the nature of angels." In Sufi phraseology the name "Jesus" seems at times not to connote personality, but to be a synonym for spirit, while the body, exactly as with St. Francis, is called "the ass" no doubt with reference to the Gospel narrative of our Lord's entry into Jerusalem. In one striking passage, of which the following is a rough but fairly literal translation, he says to one enslaved by his senses:—

"You deserted Jesus, a mere ass to feed,
Certainly, midst asses, you might take the lead!
Destiny of Jesus points to wisdom's rank,
Destiny of asses simply is—a blank.
Pity keep for Jesus, pity not the ass!
Let not fleshly impulse intellect surpass.
If an ass could somewhat catch of Jesus' mind,
Classed among the sages, he himself would find;
Though because of Jesus you may suffer woe,
Still from Him comes healing: Never let Him go"

The perusal of this and many similar passages by thoughtful Muhammadans must leave on their minds something of the effect that Matthew Arnold wished the Socratic method would have on the prejudice-bound minds of his countrymen, *i.e.*, that of inducing a fresh play of thought and feeling over their stock notions and habits.

This is not mere conjecture. Three of the above quotations were taken down by the writer from the lips of Muhammedans in the Peshawar district. It is refreshing to see in the East as in the West the poet counterworking the formalist. Another quotation heard in the Peshawar bazaar was the following "Kaleed-i-dar-i-dozakh ast ān namāz Ki barae-mardum guzāri darāz"

"The prayer thou prayest to be seen of men
Is but the key to unlock the devil's den."

Besides Jalaluddin and the other Persian poets, Ghazzali (1058-1111 A.D.), the Persian theologian, some of whose works have been translated into Pushtu, has great weight with the mullahs. He also insists on religion being a matter of the heart and not of mere external observance. He is very severe on the flippant way in which most Muhammodans used the name of God, exclaiming, "nauzub'illah" ("we take refuge in God") on the most trivial occasions. "If you see a lion coming towards you," he says, "and there is a fort close by, you do not stand exclaiming, 'I take refuge in this fort!' but you get into it. Similarly when you hear of the wrath to come, do not merely *say* 'I take refuge in God,' but take refuge in Him."

But unlike some critics he judged himself with equal severity. In his "Minqadh min ud-dalal" ("Deliverance from error"), which is one of the rare specimens of Eastern autobiography, he says, referring to the time when he was professor of theology at Bagdad: "Reflecting upon my situation I found myself bound to this world by a thousand ties; temptations assailed me on all sides. I then examined my actions. The best were those relating to instruction and education, and even there I saw myself given up to unimportant sciences, all useless in another world. Reflecting on the aim of my teaching, I found it was not pure in the sight of the Lord. I saw that all my efforts were directed towards the acquisition of glory to myself."

He left Bagdad and went into religious retirement in Syria for some years. He made a profound examination of the Sufi system, and came to the conclusion that they, as distinguished from the mere philosophers and theologians, alone understood the way to God, and that their doctrine of union with Him was no mere delusion, though they were in danger of falling into heresy in expressing it.

A third great Persian mystic, held in great repute among the Pathans, who call him "Loe Jawan" (the "Grand Young Man"), is Abdul Qadir Jilani, whose shrine at Bagdad is a great centre of pilgrimage. He was the founder of the Order of the Kadiri, widely spread in North Africa. In the Peshawar Bazaar may be purchased a broadsheet of Pushtu rhymes, extolling him in the most extravagant terms:—

> "Lofty is thy rank, O King of Bagdad!
> Help I ask from thee, O King of Bagdad!"

This fervent apostrophe of a dead saint seems a kind of unconscious witness in the Muhammadan heart to the need of a mediator.

Abdul Qadir Jilani does not seem to have been over troubled with modesty. One of his celebrated sayings is, "My foot is on the necks of all the saints of God." In a short Arabic biography of him, translated by Professor D. S. Margoliouth in the Asiatic Society's Journal, 1907, the following remarkable utterance of his is reported: "I should like to be in the desert and waste places as I was at first, neither seeing mankind nor being seen. Yet God desired to benefit mankind through me, and indeed more than five hundred persons have by me been converted to Islam, and more than 100,000 robbers and bandits been brought by me to repentance. And this is a great deal of good."

Another reported utterance of his shows that he had risen above the ordinary Muhammadan doctine of human merit and good works to apprehend something of the meaning of grace: "How can the word 'reward' or 'recompense' spring to the lips of him who has reached the higher stage of mystic perfection; who is dead to self and the creature, and all human ambitions, purposes, delights, enjoyments. His own acts of obedience of service, of worship, he regards as of God's grace alone. Verily the servant of God has no claim of right or deserving upon his Lord."

Afghan Poets

CHAPTER XIII

ONE does not generally associate the idea of poetry with Afghans, and in marked contrast to the treatment which Persian poetry has received, only two English scholars, Major Raverty and Mr. Biddulph, have troubled themselves to translate Afghan poetry into English. It is, of course, far below the lofty flights of Hafiz and Jalaludin Rumi, but it has a rude simplicity and sincerity of its own and is free both from the bombast and obscenity which often disfigures Persian poetry.

Contrary to what one might expect, Afghan poetry is highly moral and didactic, and is sometimes suggestive of Martin Tupper. Take the following, for instance, from Abdurrahman, their favourite poet (A.D. 1634)* :—

"Come, do not be the source of trouble unto any one,
For this short life of thine will soon be lost, O faithless one!

"No one is to be a tarrier behind in this world,
All are to be departers, either to-day or to-morrow."

"Those dear friends who to-day bloom before thee,
Will in two or three short days fade and decay."

Shouldst thou give but a grain of corn unto the hungry,
Verily it will hereafter be thy provision in eternity."

"Shouldst thou bestow but a drop of water on the thirsty,
It will become an ocean between thee and the fire of hell."

Like all Muhammadan poetry, Afghan verse is strongly tinged with Sufism (v. the previous chapter). Disdain-

*The translations are by Major Raverty and Mr. Biddulph.

ing outward forms and the dogmas of Muhammadanism, the Sufis aspire to a life of contemplation and fina absorption into the Deity. They believe that He is diffused through all created things and that the soul of man is part of Him. In fact they are the New Theologians of Islam. They teach that the soul of man is an exile from its Creator; that the body is its cage or prison-house, and that the term of life in this world is a period of banishment from Him. They suppose that in a prior state of existence the soul had been united with God, and that at the Creation the created spirits were summoned before the Supreme Soul, from which they emanated, when a celestial voice demanded from each separately "Alasto bi-rabbikum?" *i.e.*, "Art thou not with thy God?" to which the spirits replied "Bala"—"Yes," hence "Alasto" "Art thou not?" and "Bala" "Yes" are of constant occurrence in the mystical poems; they are the question and answer of the primeval compact; the echo of "Alasto" is always sounding in the ears of poets.

There is a regular vocabulary of the words used by these mystic poets; for instance, wine means devotion; sleep is meditation on the Divine Perfection; perfume, hope of the Divine favour; zephyrs are outbursts of divine grace; the tavern is a secluded oratory where they become intoxicated with the wine of love; beauty denotes the perfection of the deity. Mr. R. A. Nicholson, in his preface to the Diwan of Jalaluddin Rumi, has pointed out that Sufism is largely derived from the Neo-platonism of Alexandria. This accounts perhaps for the curiously Christian ring of some lines in Persian and Afghan verse composed long before the arrival of any missionary. Thus Abdurrahman says "His (Christ's) voice was the water of life to every dead man."

Afghan Poets

Abdurrahman is the most popular of the Afghan poets and deeply imbued with Sufistic doctrine. He belonged to the village of Hazar-Khana near Peshawar ; he was a man of learning and lived the life of a Dervish, absorbed in religious contemplation, separated from the world and holding no more intercourse with men than it was absolutely impossible to avoid. After the gift of poetry was bestowed upon him, he was generally found by his friends in tears ; indeed, he is said to have wept so much that his tears produced wounds in both cheeks. His strict seclusion gave rise to a report that he had turned atheist, and given up worshipping altogether ; and things would have gone hardly with him if he had not made submission and promised for the future to go to public worship and perform his devotions with the rest of the congregation. There is some dispute as to the exact period when he lived, but it was probably between the years 1634 and 1680 A.D. Some of his descendents by his daughter's side are still living, and his tomb near his native village is visited as a shrine.

The following poem, the refrain of which "Dre wara yow dee," has been taken by Mr. Kipling as the title of one of his short stories, is couched in the Sufi phraseology mentioned above.

"The face of the beloved, the sun and the moon
Are all three one.

"I have not the least need either of honey or of sugar,
For the lips of the Beloved, honey and sugar
Are all three one.

"When I am soiled with any dust of the valley she dwelleth in
This dust and musk and amber Are all three one.

"The very moment that man biddeth adieu unto the world
Dust, silver and gold unto him Are all three one.

With the Afghans

"Through the despotic severity of tyrannical rulers
The grave and hell and Peshawar
Are all three one.

"What matter though he praise himself unto Rahmān?
Still the fool, the ox and the ass
Are all three one."

The poet next to Abdurrahman in popularity is Khushal Khan, his contemporary, but of a very opposite character. He was the chief of the Khuttacks, the most polished of the Afghan tribes, and on the death of his father in a raid on the neighbouring tribe of the Yusafzais was confirmed in his fief by the Mughal emperor, Shah Jehan, who entrusted to him the responsibility of maintaining the high road from Attock to Peshawar. Khushal Khan faithfully served the emperor Shah Jehan and his successor, the bigoted Aurangzeb, who had obtained the throne by imprisoning his father and killing his brothers. Aurangzeb, as commonly with usurpers, was of a suspicious nature, and when the governor of Cabul, Khushal Khan's mortal enemy, denounced him to the emperor as guilty of disloyalty, the latter imprisoned him far from his native hills in the fort of Gwalior in Hindustan. There he languished for seven years. The following poem expresses eloquently the pangs of home-sickness which the imprisoned Afghan chieftain suffered :—

"Gentle breeze of the morn ! shouldst thou pass over Khairabad*
Or should thy course lead thee by Saraet†, on the banks of the Sind.

"Hail them again and again with my greetings and salutations,
And with them many many expressions of my regard and love.

"Cry out unto the swift Aba-Sind‡ with sonorous voice,
But unto the Landaey, mildly and whisperingly say :

*A village facing Attock on the opposite side of the Indus.

†The poet's birth-place.

‡"Father Indus," the usual name of the river among the Afghans.

"Perhaps I may drink once more a cup of thy waters,
For I was not always a dweller on Ganges' and on Jumna's banks.

"Once more, O God delight by uniting me to her again,
That heart which now from her separated is rent in twain.

"In Hind, O Khushāl thou wilt not remain for aye,
For the sinner even at last will escape from the fire of hell."

His indignation against the Emperor Aurangzeb found vent in the following:—

"I am well acquainted with Aurangzeb's justice and equity,
His orthodoxy in matters of faith—his self-denial and fasts.

"His own brothers one after the other cruelly put to the sword,
His father overcome in battle and into prison thrown.

"Tho' a person dash his head against the ground a thousand times,
Or by his fastings should bring his navel and spine together.

"Until coupled with the desire of acting with virtue and goodness
His adorations and devotions are all impositions and lies.

'The way of him whose tongue is one and the path of his heart another.
Let his very vitals be mangled and lacerated by the knife.

"Externally the serpent is handsome and symmetrically formed,
But internally is with uncleanness and with venom filled.

"Since the arm of Khushal cannot reach the tyrant here,
In the day of doom, may the Almighty have no mercy on him.

"However, in the midst of my sorrow for two things I thank God,
One, that I am an Afghan, the other that I am Khushal Khan, Khuttack."

During his imprisonment anarchy reigned on the banks of the Indus: the highway was infested by gangs of robbers, and the Mughal Government was powerless. The prisoner at Gwalior was the only man capable of restoring order. Aurangzeb issued an order for his release, summoned him to Delhi, restored his fief, and ordered him to bring the disturbed district under control. But this belated justice could not eradicate the desire for vengeance in Khushal Khan's heart; he returned to his native country entirely alienated from Aurangzeb.

The iron had entered into his soul, and he never forgot the wrongs he had suffered, as he says in one of his poems :—

> "The dark night of Aurangzeb's prison I hold in remembrance,
> When all the night long 'O God! O God!' continually I cried."

Watching his opportunity, he allied himself with the Afreedees and began a war of extermination against the Mughal Government. All the Afghan tribes as far as Jelalabad joined in the revolt. Khushal Khan hoped to weld them into one in the desire of annihilating their common foe, a dream that was realised, a century later, by Ahmed Shah the Durrani (v. chap. i.). But the eternal jealousies and rivalries of the Afghans were too strong for the Khuttack chief. He returned from an attempt to rouse the neighbouring tribe of the Yusufzais in deep chagrin and gave vent to his feelings in the following verses :—

> "I cry to them 'Arm! Arm!' till I am weary but deaf to all,
> They neither answer 'Let us die!' nor 'My life for thee!

> "The dogs of the Khattucks are worth more than the Yusufzais
> Though the Khattucks themselves are little better than dogs.

> "All the other Afghans from Candahar to Attock, openly or secretly are united to defend their honour,
> "Battles have taken place on all sides, but among the Yusufzais no spark of zeal can be kindled."

"For a year Aurangzeb has encamped before us, haggard and perplexed, his heart wounded,
"Year after year his nobles fall in the battle, and his scattered armies, who can count them?
"The treasures of India are spread out before us; his red mohurs of gold have been swallowed up in these hills
"And at a time so full of honour and glory for us as this, what are they doing, those vile traitors among the Afghans?
"The Afghans would easily beat the Mughals at sword play, if only they had a little sense.
"If the different tribes supported each other, kings would bow and prostrate themselves before them."
"I alone, among the Afghans, lament our honour and renown, while the Yusufzais cultivate their fields at ease."
'In my poor judgment death is preferable to life, when one can no longer enjoy life with honour."

But the poet's words were powerless. It was in vain that he invoked the memories of the great Pathan Kings of Delhi, Bahlol, and Shir-Shah, and preached the duty of concord. They could not understand him.

"We converse together in one tongue; we speak the Pushtu language,

"But we do not in the least understand what we to one another say."

The mohurs of gold were more effectual than the Mughal sword. One by one the tribes submitted. The two Afreedee chiefs, Amal Khan, Khushal Khan's allies, had died. The mallicks, or heads of tribes, accepted Aurangzeb's gold, and Khushal Khan, resigning the chieftainship of the Khuttucks in favour of his eldest son Ashraf, retired into private life and occupied himself with writing history, poetry, &c. He had a fairly high opinion of his own verse as appears from the following:—

"The wise know well their value, what should the fool know of them?
Pearls of speech are they which I, Khushal, have strung together.
Liars are all who say that such as I have written in Pushtu.

There are any other such verses or ever have been before.
I am not always pleased at my own verses, yet what can I do?
My heart drives me against my will, at times I am impelled to it.
For twenty years past the cauldron of my poetry has been seething,
Not till now is it fit for use, that my life has passed sixty years.
If my rival on my verses places his finger in criticism,
Whatever faults he finds I forgive him for them all,
In poetry, if there be any purport it is this,
That under cover of it the poet may tell of noble actions."

His literary retirement, however, was interrupted by troubles caused by his sons, of whom he had fifty-seven, besides several daughters. "Dogs of such description have been born unto him," he says, "I have my doubts whether Khushal is a human being at all." His second son Bahram ("Bahram the wicked") endeavoured to wrest the chieftainship from the eldest son Ashraf. The latter took him prisoner in battle, but in a weak moment set him at liberty. Bahram in return managed to betray Ashraf into the hands of the Emperor Aurangzeb, who sent him prisoner to Bijapur, where he died after ten years' captivity. Khushal Khan came out of his retreat to support the young son of Ashraf, Afzal Khan, but Bahram, supported by the Mughals, was too strong for him. He sent his son Mukarram with a body of troops to endeavour to capture his father. The old chieftain, who had attained his 77th year, advanced to meet them with his drawn sword in his hand, exclaiming, "Whoever are men amongst you, come to the sword, if ye dare." Mukarram was ashamed to lay hands on the old man and returned to his father, who was enraged at his failure, and ordered him to return and kill Khushal with his own hand if he should refuse to deliver himself up. On Mukarram's return the old chief again came out, and, taking his stand upon the crest of the hill, with his sword in his hand, again dared them to approach. He is said to have remained thus for several days.

Bahram sent a messenger to the Mughal governor at Peshawar to tell him the old lion was at length at bay, and to ask for an escort to conduct him to Peshawar. Khushal, however, having been warned, made his escape, and took refuge in the Afreedee country, where he died in the 78th year of his age.

Before his decease he charged those sons who were with him to bury him where "the dust of the hoofs of the Mughal cavalry might not light on his grave," and if they should succeed at any time in capturing Bahram the Malignant they should divide his body into two parts and burn one half at the head of his grave and the other at the foot. He was buried at a small hamlet named I-surraey in the Khuttuck hills, where his tomb still exists.

There is something in Khushal Khan's character and circumstances, his poetic faculty, his courage against his country's enemies, his susceptibility to the fair sex, his vindictiveness, and his rebellious children, which not very remotely recalls that of David. He certainly had more conscience than the average Afghan, as appears from the following:—

"The carnality of my heart is an Afreedee who for religion careth not—"

"Its good thoughts are but few; but unto wickedness it is exceedingly prone."

"Like unto Akhund Darwezah* I point out godliness and piety to it."

"But the flesh teacheth it impiety and infidelity like unto Pir Roshan."*

"Two and sixty years by computation my own age hath now reached."

"And my black hair hath turned silvery, but my heart no the least white."

*V. Chap. iv. "The Religion of the Pathans."

His large experience of the opposite sex had not left him with a high opinion of them :—

"All women are of intellect deficient.
And the voluntary cause of life's ills."

"Thou mays't be straight and even with them,
But they are crooked and wayward with thee."

"Do them a thousand benefits and services,
Yet, at a single word, their hearts sulky grow."

"They become poison unto thee and kill thee,
They, whom thou deemest a healing balm."

"They have no fidelity in their composition,
They are naturally unto perfidiousness prone."

"Created indeed in the figure of mankind,
But, in reality, with no humanity in them."

"They make thee out culpable upon a slight offence,
But they cannot be wrong however great their sins.

"Say no more about them, O Khushal,
It would be better had they never existed."

He suspected the Sufis :—

"The believers in Sufi mystics and the unbelievers are all one,"

was hard on the orthodox mullah,

"A hundred beads on his rosary, a hundred sins in his heart,"

and bitterly expressed his sense of the perfidy of his fellow-countrymen :—

"Verily the Afghans are deficient in sense and understanding.
They are the tail-cut curs of the butcher's slaughter-house.
They have played away Dominion for the gold of the Mughals.
And they lust after the offices that the Mughals can give.

Though the camel with its lading hath entered their dwelling
They are first taken up with stealing the bell from its neck.
Out upon him who first the name of Sarrah-bān* bore!
And malediction upon the whole of them that after follow!
They commence from Candahar and reach unto Damghār." †
And all are worthless and good for nothing who dwell between.

But at times his grimness would relax into a "carpe diem" mood:—

"If the sword is sharpened, is it not made sharp to smite?
If the locks are curlèd, are they not for love's delight?
Tell me not, O preacher, not to gaze upon the rose
What were eyes designed for, but to look with, I suppose!
Let the mullah fast, but let me quaff the crimson wine,
Every creature acts his part, and I no less act mine."

No other figures on the rugged Afghan Parnassus stand out with greater distinctness than Abdurrahman and Khushal Khan, but Pushtu poems are still extant from the hand of Ahmed Shah, the conqueror of the Mahrattas and the grandfather of Shah Shujah, whose restoration to the throne of Cabul by the British led to the first Afghan War.

There remain the "dums" or wandering minstrels who, as mentioned in the chapter on village itineration (c. 6), compose war narratives exulting over the defeats of the English by the Afghans. The late Professor Darmesteter published an interesting account of these "dums" in the "Contemporary Review," 1888. Some recent "dum" ballads referring to the Waziri expedition of 1894 were published in the Royal Asiatic Society's Journal for 1907 by Mr. E. B. Howell. Two of the stanzas run as follows:—

"The martyrs (gazis) fought a battle. The lord priest‡

*The ancestor of the Yusufzais. †A small town in Swat.

‡The notorious Mullah Powindah, who instigated the Waziri revolt

is their commander. Harm him not, O God; he is a fragrant tree of the high hills. He has bound the English in chains; the English women are affrighted in London."

"The martyrs fought a battle; my Tilak was full of heart when he went up upon a great English infidel. Look you, my friends, in his hand was a dagger; look, he has stricken that fat Englishman on the arm."

The whole poem reminds me strongly of the song of Deborah and Barak.

A few words may be added on Pushtu, the Afghan language. It is not so harsh as is sometimes supposed. It is true Mohammed is said, when he heard it, to have called it "the language of hell," but observing that his Afghan interlocutor was annoyed, he appeased him by using it and saying, "Ghashe linde rawra" ("Bring my bow and arrows"). A line like this, which we find in the first poem of Abdurrahman, is certainly not unrhythmical nor unmusical:—

> "Tal tar tala barqarar dai Rabb zamā."
> "Everlastingly the same is my God."

Apart from its poetry, Afghan literature is mostly imitative. Numerous tales in verse and prose have been translated from Persian into Pushtu, such as the Yusuf and Zulaikha of Jami and part of the Gulistan of Saadi. Theological works are also numerous, the principal being the "Makhzan-i-Pushtu" of Akhund Darwezah, which is the earliest work extant in the language. It is particularly interesting historically as written to controvert the doctrines of the Roshenia sect (v. chap 6), which, if it had not been so stoutly opposed, would have probably spread throughout the length and breadth of Afghanistan. Pir Roshan ("the saint of light"), whose name his opponent, Akhund Darwezah, changed into "Pir Tarik" ("the saint of darkness"), was an Afghan Sufi, who proclaimed him self to be a prophet and aimed at the establishment of a new faith (circ 1540 A.D.). His celebrated work was the "Khair ul bayan," written in Arabic, Persian, Hindustani, and Pushtu, and said by him, unlike the Koran, to have been received directly from the Almighty without the intervention of the Archangel Gabriel. One of his Pushtu couplets is generally quoted as a proof of the heretical nature of his tenets; it runs as follows:—

"Māl o mulk warah de Khuda dé
Da halāl harām rāghle de kumah."

"Property and kingdom all are of God,
This 'lawful and unlawful,' whence came they?

Afghan Fables

CHAPTER XIV

Translated by permission from a collection of Pushtu tales made by MOOLLAH AHMAD, *of Tungi, under the direction of the* REV. H. P. HUGHES, *late missionary at Peshawar* (1865-1884).

1. HOIST WITH HIS OWN PETARD

A CERTAIN man with a propensity for preaching used to go daily into a king's court and say in a loud voice, "Do good to the good, and let the bad punish themselves." One of the courtiers took umbrage at this, and determined somehow to get him forbidden entrance. So he went to the king and said, "Please, your Majesty! The preacher who frequents your court spreads among the common people the report that your Majesty's breath is malodorous." The king was very angry, and said, "How do you know that?" "The next time he comes," replied the slanderer, "call him to come near, and you will see how he lays his hand upon his mouth." "Very well," said the king, "I will find out." The same day the slanderer invited the preacher to lunch, and took care that strong onions should form part of the repast. After lunch the preacher betook himself as usual to the court, and proclaimed again, "Do good to the good, and let the bad punish themselves." "Come here, my friend," said the king, looking at him in anything but a friendly manner. As the man approached he laid his hand on his mouth that the king might not be annoyed by his onion-scented breath. The king felt certain that the slanderer's assertion was true, and immediately sent off a letter to his vizier by the hand of the preacher, in which he wrote, "On receipt of this flay the bearer alive; stuff his skin with straw and send it back." As a rule when the king sent anyone with a letter to his vizier it was generally to be paid a reward. Knowing this, the slanderer hastened after his victim and offered to take the note for him. "Certainly," replied the other, so the slanderer set off post-haste to the vizier.

As soon as the latter had read the note he immediately sent for the executioner and ordered the slanderer to strip. "Why?" faltered the astounded man, turning pale. The vizier said, "The king commands me to kill the bearer of this letter." "Wait a minute," said the slanderer, "that was intended for someone else." "The letter says nothing about 'wait a minute!'" the vizier replied, "Executioner, perform your duty." Accordingly the man was beheaded on the spot, and his skin stuffed with straw and sent to the king. The next day the preacher, according to his wont, came to the court and renewed his cry, "Do good to the good, and let the bad punish themselves." The king was astonished, and said to him, "What have you done with my letter?" The preacher replied, "Your Majesty, one of your courtiers offered to take it for me, so I gave it to him." The king asked, "Did you say that my breath was malodorous?" "Heaven is witness, such a thought never crossed my mind," returned the trembling preacher. "Why, then, did you lay your hand on your mouth that day I summoned you to approach me?" the king inquired. "That was because I had eaten onions, and I did not wish your Majesty to be annoyed by the smell of them." "Very well," replied the pacified monarch, "preach away, for your sermon has truth in it."

2. "Whatsoever a man Soweth."

The ancients relate that Luqman the wise in his youth was a slave of an uncomely aspect. On one occasion when exposed for sale in the bazaar he was purchased by a farmer, who took him home. On the first night when the third watch was passed Luqman came to his master and said (1) "Sir! rise and pray, if you wish to win heaven and escape hell." His master replied, "Let me sleep a bit. The Lord is merciful." When the fourth watch was past, while it was yet dark Luqman came again and said, "Rise, master! if you want to lay up a store of merit for the next world." "Go away," he growled, "I'm sleepy; God is gracious." When the morning light dawned Luqman, came the third time and said, "Master, man and beast are everyone of them worshipping God: now is the time to sow devoutness if you have any." "Just a little more sleep," his master murmured, "then I will get up." When at last the farmer rose, he delivered to Luqman the plough, the ox-yoke, and all the necessary implements together with a basket of barley-seed, and said to him, "Go to such a place and they will show you my field: plough it with even furrows, and sow this barley in them: work till I come presently, and if I don't come work all the same, and then come home." "Very well," said Luqman, and went off. On the way, however, he entered a neighbour's house and exchanged the barley for some millet. Arrived at the field he ploughed it and sowed the millet in the furrows. Then, as his master had not come, he went home.

After some time had elapsed his master said to him, "Come! Luqman, let us go and look at the field which you sowed." Luqman said, "Very well, sir," so they

(1) Devout Mohammedans pray often at night as well as by day

both went together. When they got to the field the farmer stared and stared, but not a blade of barley could he see. "Luqman," he said, "those little green sprouts that are coming up are not barley but some other kind of crop." "Yes, master," replied Luqman, "they are millet; I never sowed the barley." "What!" shouted the farmer, "I gave you barley to sow, and you sowed millet!" "Keep cool, master," returned the imperturbable Luqman. "God is merciful; doubtless it will turn into barley," His master said, "Certainly God is merciful, but you sowed millet; how can you expect to reap barley?" "With just as much right, sir," replied Luqman, "as you, who sleep with sluggards, expect to soar with saints."

3. The Lion and the Beasts.

A certain jungle was once haunted by a lion, who held all the other animals in awe, and carried them off whenever he chose. At last the animals held a meeting and said to each other, "It will be better if we cast lots as to who shall be the lion's dinner each day, so that the rest may for a short time at least be free from fear." They called the lion and told him of their proposal, to which he, after some hesitation, consented. Accordingly each day, whatever animal was chosen by lot made his way to the lion while the rest roamed at large, free from anxiety.

At last it came to the hare's turn. Instead of going forthwith, however, he said to his fellow animals: "I have a scheme for ridding ourselves of this tyrant." They asked him to tell it, but he refused and set off with deliberate delay to the lion's den. Arrived there he found the royal beast fretting and fuming at the delay in the arrival of his food. When he caught sight of the hare the lion frowned and said, "Despicable scoundrel, why have you delayed so long? I made this agreement with you, and now you animals are trying to cheat me altogether. When I am nearly worn out with waiting they send a miserable fragment like yourself." In a trembling voice the hare said, "Your majesty, I have an explanation to make if your majesty will vouchsafe to hear it." "Explain then!" growled the lion, "and be quick about it." "This morning," went on the hare, my companion and myself started as in duty bound to provide your majesty with a breakfast. On the road we encountered another lion, who bade us halt at peril of our lives. Notwithstanding all my protests that we were your majesty's subjects, he insisted on detaining my companion, and I fear your future meals will be much diminished unless your majesty goes to clear the road of this robber." "Ha! where is he? Lead me to him," roared the lion in a greater rage than before. Accordingly they went on, the lion leading the way.

Presently the hare slunk behind. "Where are you going now?" demanded the lion. "Please your majesty," replied the hare, "we are now approaching the well where the monster lives. I feel too nervous to go any nearer alone, but if your majesty will condescend to let me sit on your shoulders I will point him out to you." When the lion got to the well he looked down and saw his own angry face glaring up at him from the clear water. "Certainly," he growled, "there he is!" Accordingly he jumped in, the hare leapt off his back, and the water closed placidly over the head of the too credulous lion.

4. The Merchant and the Parrot.

A merchant once intending to travel to Hindustan asked all the inmates of his house, small and great, what tokens he should bring them thence as keepsakes. Each commissioned the merchant to bring something he had set his mind upon. Among the rest was a parrot from India who had been long confined in a cage. To him the merchant came in turn and said, "Well, Polly, what shall I bring you from your native land?" The parrot replied, "Kindly go to such a place where the parrots are flying free in the woods and say to them, 'Your old comrade sends you a message by me, and asks if you have forgotten your old friend immured in a cage while you fly about at liberty?'" "Certainly," said the merchant, "I will do so with pleasure."

After he had executed his other commissions in India, he remembered his promise, and went to the place mentioned where the parrots were flying about the trees. He delivered the message, but no sooner had he done so than to his consternation one of the parrots began to flutter as if stricken by an arrow, and then fell to the ground, stone dead. The astonished merchant said to himself, "Certainly there must have been some strong tie of kinship or friendship between that bird and mine."

After finishing his business in India he returned home, and to the delight of all distributed the various presents he had brought. At last he came to the parrot, sitting disconsolate in its cage. No sooner had he told the bird his story than it fluttered and fell stone dead in its cage precisely as the other had done. The merchant wrung his hands with grief, as the bird was a favourite of his. He drew its body out of the cage and threw it away. To his amazement no sooner had it touched the ground than it flew upwards and perched on the branch of a tree. The merchant stared at it and said, "In Allah's name, what is the meaning of this?" "My friend in India," the parrot replied, "had sent me a message, which you did not understand, to the intent that if I played the part of a dead bird I would win my liberty. I took his advice and won it, as you see; but as I have eaten your salt, I ask you kindly to pardon me." The merchant replied, "Yes, I forgive you; go in peace."

5. Dangerous Friendship.

One day a young man on his walks abroad saw a bear and a gigantic boa-constrictor locked in deadly conflict, the bear evidently being near his last gasp. The young man drew his sword, and running up killed the snake and delivered the bear. Thereupon the latter, full of gratitude, attached himself closely to the youth and followed him assiduously wherever he went.

On one occasion while the youth was asleep, and the bear sitting by watching over him, a man came up and seeing the pair, roused the youth from slumber and said, "Young man, what have you to do with that bear?" The youth told him the story of their friendship, whereupon the man proceeded. "Yes, that is a pretty story, but it is likely to be a dangerous friendship." "Oh, go on," said the youth, "don't bother me! I'm sleepy." The man persisted in his warnings, but only meeting with rebuffs, went somewhat sadly upon his way. When he had gone the youth resumed his slumbers, and the bear continued to sit by him watching. By chance a fly came and settled on the sleeper's face. The bear with a clumsy movement of his paw whisked it off; this happened several times, but the fly always pertinaciously returned to the attack. At last the bear, losing patience, seized a large stone, and crushed both the fly and the face of his friend.

6. The Unequal Yoke.

A frog and a mouse had once struck up a great friendship, and their love increased as time went on. One day the mouse said to the frog, "My friend, it is very awkward when I come down to the water-side, and call to you and you cannot hear, because you are under the water. I am so fond of you that I am not satisfied with seeing you only occasionally." "Well you know," replied the frog, "they say 'Absence makes the heart grow fonder.'" "Cold-blooded creature!" returned the mouse, "my heart can't grow any fonder than it is already. Let us have a go-between to carry messages, or some way of signalling to each other when we want to." "Very well," said the frog, "suppose we get a string and tie one end to your leg and the other to mine; when you want me, or I want you, we can each twitch our own end of the string." A frog who overheard them said "Perhaps your plan will entail some inconvenience; suppose each of you want to go a different way?" "Hold your tongue," they cried, "you are only envious of our friendship." "Very well," he replied, "do as you like." To every similar suggestion of possible difficulty made by others of their friends they turned a deaf ear. "We are now one," they said, "for better, for worse."

One day a hawk swooped down on the mouse. The mouse scuttled, but being hampered by the string, could not go fast enough and was caught and carried up into the air, while the unfortunate frog dangled from the other end of the string. Some people in a village over which the hawk was passing saw the frog dangling and said, "See! what an extraordinary clever hawk! How did he manage to catch the frog?" "He is not extraordinarily clever," replied the frog, "but we were extraordinarily foolish for not listening to advice."

7. The Sick Man, The Qazi and the Saint.

One day a physician came to a sick man and laying his finger on his pulse ascertained that he was very ill. From further inquiry he found that he could neither eat with relish, nor had any pleasure in life. Determined to rouse him if possible to shake off his lethargy, he said "Well, the best advice I can give you is to eat what you like, walk where you like, and above all, don't worry." The patient, pleased at being released from rules, went to take the air by the riverside. There he saw a "saint" or "sheikh" busily occupied in his ablutions. The saint's neck being smooth and fat, presented a very tempting object for a slap, and remembering the doctor's advice not to deny himself anything he fancied, the sick man stole up behind him and gave him a resounding slap on the neck. "Hullo," exclaimed the saint, "what did you strike me for?" At first he thought of requiting him in kind, but noticing his sickly appearance, he thought better of it and carried him before a judge. "Judge," he said, "this man struck me on the neck absolutely without provocation, now therefore kindly blacken his face, have him mounted on an ass with his face to the tail,* and let him be led through the bazaars." "Don't be angry, Sheikh," said the judge, "that poor fellow looks too weak to have done you much harm: rather you ought to give him an alms if you can afford it; everyone expects a saint to return good for evil." The saint said "I have only six rupees in all the world." "Well," said the judge, "you should give him three."

While they were talking the sick man's attention was attracted by the judge's neck, which was also smooth and fat. Again he yielded to the temptation, and stealing up quietly, delivered him a resounding slap. "Let me have the six rupees," he said, "and let me go! I am too weak to stand here all day long." The judge flushed up and grew purple with wrath, while the saint saw his oppor-

*A common Mohammedan punishment.

tunity and said, " 'Tis strange justice, judge, that you bid me requite evil with good, and when your turn comes to exhibit saintliness, you look like an enraged turkeycock. Suppose, now you give him an alms in accordance with your own precepts." "The fact is, Sheikh," the judge replied, trying to smooth down his ruffled dignity, "I was really at heart very pleased at being struck." "It looks like it," the saint remarked sardonically, "I suppose that is why you clenched your fist and your eyes watered; of course I can't see your heart." "Eye-water makes the heart blossom" sententiously returned the Qazi. "If it were not for scoundrels we could not distinguish saints: if it were not for pebbles, no one would value pearls; if it were not for cowards, who would crown heroes? and if you and I do not forgive this man who has injured us, wherein do we differ from common folk?" "That's so," replied the saint, and together they dismissed the sick man richer by six rupees and their benediction.

8. Sultan Mahmoud and the Thieves.

Sultan Mahmoud, of Ghazni, had the habit of going among the meanest of the people at night, clothed in poor apparel, in order to ascertain their condition. One night he found himself near a gang of thieves. They saw him approaching and called out, "Who are you?" "One of yourselves," he replied. Accordingly they invited him to sit down with them.

Presently each of them began describing his own special proficiency in the art of burgling, previous to making an expedition. The first said, "I understand exactly what a dog says when he barks;" the second, "I can recognise a man in the dark, however far off he may be, and can identify him by day;" the third said "I am an adept at boring through walls "*; the fourth, "I have an extremely keen scent for buried treasures;" the fifth, "I can fling a rope ladder on a wall, so that however high and smooth the wall may be, it will catch hold."

When each had severally described his proficiency they turned to the king and said, "Well, young man, are you good for anything but carrying our bundles?" "Yes," replied the disguised monarch, "I have such power that when a number of men are prisoners, and sentence of execution has been passed upon them and the executioner is standing by with a drawn sword in his hand, if but a hair of my beard wags, they all go free." "Bravo!" they exclaimed, "you are the man for us! You shall be our king." They then went out and made for a strongly fortified building, where they heard a dog barking. The man learned in dog-language said, "His bark signifies that the king is with us." "Of course he is with us" they replied, "did not we make him king? What other do we need?" Then the keen-scented man said "Certainly I smell treasure here." The adept in flinging the rope ladder brought his art into play; they all scaled the wall, made their way into the treasure-house by the help of the "jemmy"-wielder, brought out an immense amount of treasure, and buried it. They then appointed a night for meeting to divide the treasure and went their various ways, the king going home to his palace, but not till he had ascertained the name and abode of each. Next morning he gave orders to his chief police officer to have them brought before him. Immediately the man endowed with keen vision recognised the king and said to his fellows "That is our comrade of last night!" They then simultaneously went on their knees to the king and begged

*The common form of burglary in the East, the walls being mostly made of dried mud.

permission to urge one request, which he granted. "Your majesty," they said, "You have just seen one of us exhibit the skill he claimed to have in recognising your majesty, but there was another among us who claimed to have a wonderful power of setting prisoners free, and *that* claim still waits for verification." The king, rather than give the lie to his own claim, ordered them to be set free, and awarded them as large a sum out of his treasury as might suffice to secure them for the future from the necessity of living by thievery.

9. Courtship and Afterwards.

A falcon once circling high in the air and surveying all beneath him, spied a red-legged partidge. So graceful was her gait and so sweet her voice that he fell violently in love with her. When the partridge saw him approaching, however, she ran as fast as she could and entered a crevice in the rocks where the falcon could not reach her. He came, however, to the mouth of the crevice and said, "O partridge, I did not know how beautiful you were; don't be frightened of me, please; let us take a stroll together." The partridge, all in a flutter, replied, "Sir, pray seek some other companion; we have no more in common than fire and water." The falcon, not to be rebuffed, replied, "Partridge, consider my motives in speaking these gentle words. My talons are not broken that I cannot hunt, nor my beak blunted that I cannot feed; it is only pure affection which prompts my utterance, you will derive many benefits from my society—first you will be safe from all other falcons, secondly I will take you to my nest, where you will live at a pitch of elevation above all other partridges, and there are many other benefits too numerous to mention." The partridge replied, "You are the king of birds, and my family are low in rank; perhaps some day if I say something disrespectful to you I shall have to suffer for it." The falcon replied, "Ah, don't you know that love is blind, and sees no faults in the beloved? I shall be so happy in your love that you can say what you like." After the partridge had exhausted all her objections, the assiduity of the falcon prevailed and he carried her off with him to his lofty nest, where they lived for a long time in peace and happiness.

But after a while the partridge, growing familiar with her consort, dropped her deferential manner. This he noticed and secretly resented, but said nothing about it, though it rankled in his mind. One day, being indisposed, he had remained in his nest without going after any prey. When night came he was exceedingly hungry, and as the partridge noticed with alarm, excessively morose and sullen. "Alas!" thought she, "It is all up with me now! Would that I had not suffered myself to be over-persuaded."

In the meantime the falcon sat aloof gloomily revolving some pretext for picking a quarrel. At last he said, "Partridge, this is a pretty arrangement that I am sweltering in the sun and you are reclining in the shade." "My dear," replied the partridge, "you seem to forget that it is night; how can you then be sitting in the sun?" "Oh, you want to argue, do you?" screamed the falcon in a fury, "I'll teach you how to argue!" So saying he fell upon her, tore her to pieces, and devoured her.